Leading Through
a Crisis

Leading Through a Crisis

Harvard Business Press

Boston, Massachusetts

13 12 11 10 09   5 4 3 2 1

Content in this book was previously published in *Leading People, Managing Crises*, and *Making Decisions* © Harvard Business School Publishing Corporation, 2006–2008

Library of Congress Cataloging-in-Publication Data
Leading through a crisis.
    p. cm.
 ISBN 978-1-4221-2965-4 (pbk.)
 1. Leadership. 2. Crisis management. I. Harvard Business School. Press.
 HD57.7.L43758 2009
 658.4'092—dc22

                          2009010480

The paper used in this publication meets the requirements of the American National Standard for Permanence of Paper for Publications and Documents in Libraries and Archives Z39.48-1992

Contents

Introduction   ix

Part I: Leading People   1

The Challenge of Contemporary Leadership   3

What Makes an Effective Leader?   7

How to Acquire Leadership Skills   17

How to Craft a Vision   25

How to Motivate the People You Need   35

How to Care for Yourself   47

Part II: Managing Crises   51

What Is a Crisis?   53

Stage 1: Avoiding the Crisis   63

Stage 2: Preparing to Manage the Crisis   69

Stage 3: Recognizing the Crisis   77

Stage 4: Containing the Crisis   83

Stage 5: Resolving the Crisis   91

Stage 6: Learning from the Crisis   99

Part III: Making Decisions   105

What Is Decision Making?   107

Step 1: Setting the Stage   111

Step 2: Recognizing Obstacles   121

Step 3: Framing the Issue at Hand   127

Step 4: Generating Alternatives   135

Step 5: Evaluating Alternatives   141

Step 6: Making the Decision   151

Step 7: Communicating the Decision   157

Step 8: Implementing the Decision   161

Assessing Your Decision-Making Process   167

Tools and Resources   175

Tools and Resources for Leading People   177

Tools and Resources for Managing Crises   207

Tools and Resources for Making Decisions   227

About the Subject Experts   254

Introduction

The word *leader* evokes images of great men and women who, in moments of crisis, rise up to make a great difference in the course of human events. Simply defined, leading is the ability to influence others to move toward the accomplishments of common goals. Every day, mothers and fathers lead, little children lead, unit heads lead.

But in a time of crisis, leadership is particularly challenging. It is the individuals who rise to this challenge whose stories we read about in books, see in films, and relate to future generations.

You probably already do lead. Think about the times recently when you have influenced others by the decisions you made, by how you chose to spend your time and money, or by simply engaging in a conversation that affected what others were doing. But how do you lead *better*, and how do you translate and grow those skills to lead better in a crisis?

In business, many people think of crisis management as a job for internal audit groups, senior executives, and public relations professionals. And it's true in part—crises such as product tampering, food contamination, or fraudulent earnings reports are best handled by these people. But there are other, broader events like today's financial crisis that could have a devastating impact on your group and organization. These may make it difficult or impossible for you to carry out your business operations—and it's up to you to make the decisions that steer your group in the right direction.

Where does a good leader begin? Start with the purpose. It does very little good to spend time trying to influence others if you have no idea for what purpose. What is the vision? Where are you trying to go? What are you trying to accomplish? This sounds so simple, but it is absolutely critical. Good leaders know what they are trying to accomplish. Part I of this book, "Leading People," will guide you through the skills you need to become a better leader, especially crafting a vision and motivating the people around you to work toward that vision.

Good leaders also have a plan to go with that sense of purpose, especially in a crisis. With good planning, you can minimize the impact of a potential disaster, avoid one altogether, or—in some cases—even help your company benefit from a crisis. Part II of this book, "Managing Crises," focuses on the skills you need to manage in a crisis, whether it be today's economic realities or some other event entirely.

Finally, leaders in a crisis must need to know how to make effective decisions. You have to know how to evaluate trade-offs, generate alternatives, and come to your final choice quickly. The path you choose will have a real impact on your company and its people, and the higher the stakes in the business world, the more charged the decision-making process becomes. During a crisis, there are many decisions to be made, and a lot rides on every choice. Part III, "Making Decisions," focuses on your skills as a decision maker, guiding you through eight steps that take the mystery out of the process of making a choice.

Let this guide help you to take the risk and be the leader you already are. In times of crisis, people are looking for a leader—all you have to do is step out and say to yourself, "OK, I am in charge, and I know where I want to go." Then say to the others, "Follow me."

Leading
People

The Challenge of Contemporary Leadership

*The definition
of leadership is to have inspired,
energized followers.*
—Warren G. Bennis

eadership used to be viewed as innate. Epitomized by heroic, Lone Ranger types, it was seen as a mystical blend of courage, charisma, and even a flair for the dramatic. But beyond those traits, to paraphrase Louis Armstrong, if you had to ask what leadership was, you'd never know.

Fortunately, we've all grown wiser—or at least, we've had the lesson drummed into us by a business climate that is increasingly competitive and volatile. Yes, leadership still calls for courage and decisiveness in the face of conflicting demands. For example, the ability to make tradeoffs between people, resources, money, and deadlines—often causing short-term pain for the sake of long-term benefit—remains a vital element of effective leadership. But the changing structure of organizations, the growth of alliances and joint ventures between organizations, indeed, the changing nature of work itself—all call for more practical and diverse approaches to leadership.

Expand your leadership skills

There will always be a time and place for charismatic leaders, but few leaders today use formal authority and the power to command and control; rather, they *influence* and *motivate* people to achieve clearly defined goals. The power to influence and motivate requires skills such as:

- Communication skills to speak and write persuasively

- Interpersonal skills to listen and hear what people are really saying

- Conflict-resolution skills to handle the inevitable times of friction and tension

- Negotiation skills to bring differing groups together

- Motivational skills to convince people to strive for the same goal

Management versus Leadership Skills

MANAGEMENT SKILLS	LEADERSHIP SKILLS
Planning and budgeting	Setting a direction
Organizing and staffing	Aligning people to a vision
Controlling and problem solving	Motivating and inspiring

Leading or managing?

Are leadership skills the same skills effective managers use? Yes, to a degree. Managing and leading are complementary and often overlapping activities. The primary difference is that managing involves coping with complexity; leading, coping with *change*. At the same time, managing requires leadership skills, and leading requires management skills.

Management skills will always be essential, but in responding and adapting to the changing socioeconomic realities of today's markets, managers, even middle managers, are increasingly being called upon to be leaders as well.

Recognize the leadership challenge

No matter what the current economic, political, and social realities may be, the challenge for leaders today is to define their special goals or vision, to acquire as many management and leadership skills as possible, and, finally, to know when to use them to influence others to reach those goals.

What Makes an Effective Leader?

The cult of the heroic leader remains strong.

—Loren Gary, editor

E ffective leaders are not born with the gift of knowing how to lead. Rather, they gain experience, they absorb knowledge, they see and listen to the world around them—both inside the organization and beyond. Effective leaders are also capable of assuming the leadership qualities needed for specific situations. There are many kinds of effective leaders—among them the charismatic leader, the transformational leader, and the pragmatic leader—but these distinctive qualities can blend together in one person in different ways at different times.

Charismatic leaders seem to shine

A charismatic leader may seem to be born with a gift to inspire. Particularly during a crisis, people turn to this powerful voice for a grand vision and hope for solutions. Such a leader can clarify the situation for his people and instill the confidence they need. People feel safe handing off a problem to this type of leader.

What makes charismatic leaders such champions? They differ from the norm in greater self-confidence, energy, enthusiasm, and unconventional behavior. Charismatic leaders tend to:

- have a clear, fresh, new, and creative vision

- be completely devoted to their vision

- make great sacrifices to achieve their vision, taking personal risks—financial, professional, social

- create a sense of urgency among their followers

- gain the absolute trust of their followers (and also fear)

- use persuasion rather than forceful commands or democratic appeals for consensus to influence their followers

A charismatic leader is most successful during a crisis. For example, Franklin Delano Roosevelt was a charismatic leader who led the United States out of the Great Depression and readied the nation for World War II. On the other hand, Adolf Hitler was also a charismatic leader who gave his defeated nation a new vision of power and might. Thus, charismatic leaders can have great power and influence, but how they use it determines whether their inspiration works for good or not.

However, most organizations are not in a continual state of peril. A lofty vision for achieving a grand mission may not be attainable, and the value of inspiration may dissolve into a need for everyday, step-by-step progress. Thus, charismatic leaders are not always the best type of leader.

"[The charismatic leader is] supposed to have the 'gift of tongues,' with which he [can] inspire employees to work harder and gain the confidence of investors, analysts, and the ever skeptical press."
—Rakesh Khurana, professor

Transformational leaders focus on the people and the task

Unlike charismatic leaders, transformational leaders remold an organization not through the force of their own personality but by appealing to their people, gaining their trust and respect. Transformational leaders achieve results by paying close attention to their group or team as they

- articulate a clear and compelling vision

- clarify the importance of the vision's outcome

- provide a well-defined path to attain the vision

- use symbols to realize their vision

- act with confidence, optimism, and self-determination

- encourage their people to work as a team rather than as individuals to reach the organization's goals

- empower people to make good decisions for the benfit of the whole

What makes transformational leaders effective is their ability to make their vision a clear, identifiable goal that can guide their team's actions to meet that goal. They trust their people, provide the resources they need, and encourage them to move forward.

"It was Sacagawea, a Shoshone teenager, who led the Lewis and Clark expedition over its most perilous routes. But you also have to remember that Lewis must have been a great leader also, because he was willing to turn over the leadership and follow a young Indian who seemed to know what she was doing, but whom he had never met before."
—Douglas T. Hall, Director of the Executive Development Roundtable

Pragmatic leaders—from the ideal to the real

The most apparent characteristic of pragmatic leaders is their focus on the organization rather than on people. Pragmatic leaders face the realities of business environment; they listen to and understand the truth, whether good or bad, hopeful or daunting. They are effective because they

- have a vision that is recognizable as a variation of the status quo

- listen carefully to their people

- make realistic decisions for the good of the organization

- manage by the numbers

- put the right people in the right positions to get the job done

- delegate responsibilities to people they can trust

Pragmatic leaders may not be as flamboyant or exciting as other types of leaders, but they get the job done. Pragmatic leaders are most effective when an organization is going through rough times or when the business environment is too turbulent to see far ahead, when a short-term, familiar vision is necessary.

After all, Meriwether Lewis and William Clark were successful in attaining the goal of their Northwest journey. When they reached the Pacific Ocean in April 1805, Lewis wrote that he was "much pleased at having arrived at this long wished for spot."

Effective leaders are future-focused

In general, leaders who are effective now and in the future have learned how to be:

- future-focused. They create a vision, articulate it to their group, and stick with it. They understand how their unit or organization fits into the larger picture, and they organize short-term tasks according to long-term priorities.

- comfortable with ambiguity. They are willing to take calculated risks, can handle a certain level of disruption and conflict, and are willing to change their minds when new information comes to light.

- persistent. They can maintain a positive, focused determination in pursuing a goal or vision, despite the obstacles.

- excellent communicators. They know how to write clearly, listen closely, run meetings, make presentations, negotiate, and speak in public.

- politically astute. They have acquired a solid sense of their organization's power structure, listen carefully to the concerns of its most powerful groups, and know where to turn for the support and resources they need.

- level-headed. They know how to stay calm in the midst of turmoil and confusion.

- self-aware. They know themselves enough to realize how their own patterns of behavior affect others.

- caring. They have a demonstrated ability to empathize with other people's needs, concerns, and professional goals.

- humorous. When the situation warrants it, they know how to inject a little mirth to relieve tension within a group.

Tip: Be the change you want to bring about—model the behaviors you're trying to encourage.

Self-Evaluation: Characteristics of Effective Leadership

The questions below relate to characteristics of effective leaders. Use the questions to evaluate whether you possess these characteristics. Use the results to see where you might focus to strengthen your leadership skills.

Characteristics of Effective Leaders	Yes	No
Future-focused		
1. Do you have a clear vision?	✓	
2. Have you made your vision clear to your group?	✓	
Persistent; tenacious		
3. When pursuing a goal, do you maintain a positive, focused attitude, despite obstacles?	✓	
Comfortable with ambiguity		
4. Are you willing to take calculated risks?	✓	
5. Are you comfortable with a certain level of disruption and conflict?	✓	
Excellent communicators		
6. Do you listen closely (rather than have a response ready before the other person finishes)?		✓
7. Are you comfortable running meetings?	✓	
8. Are you comfortable making presentations and speaking in public?	✓	
9. Do you have the skills needed to negotiate in a variety of settings?		✓
Politically astute		
10. Could you diagram for yourself your organization's actual power structure?	✓	
11. Can you articulate the concerns of your organization's most powerful groups?	✓	

Characteristics of Effective Leaders	Yes	No
12. Can you identify those individuals within your organization who will support you when needed?	✓	
13. Do you know where to turn for the resources you need?	✓	
Self-aware		
14. Are you aware of or can you describe how your own patterns of behavior affect others?		✓
Level-headed		
15. In situations that are full of turmoil and confusion, do you stay calm and level-headed?		✓
Caring		
16. Do you empathize with other people's needs, concerns, and professional goals?		✓
17. Would staff members confirm that you show such empathy?		✓
Able to use humor		
18. Do you know how to use humor to relieve tense or uncomfortable situations?	✓	

*If you answered **"yes"** to most of these questions, you have the characteristics of an effective leader.*

*If you answered **"no"** to some or many of these questions, you may want to consider how you can further develop these effective leadership characteristics.*

How to Acquire Leadership Skills

Becoming a leader does not occur by osmosis. If you want to be a leader, you need to work at it. You probably have some of the skills mastered already. You may have excellent communication skills, or you already have a pretty good idea of what your vision is. You may even have that gift to inspire others. But if you lack some skills, knowledge, or experience, go out and get them!

Be aggressive about becoming a leader

How? Here are some suggestions:

Enroll in formal leadership programs. There are plenty of management training programs; aim for the ones designed specifically for leaders. Offered by consulting companies or universities, these programs may include focused weekend workshops or yearlong programs that cover the whole range of leadership skills. The training techniques may vary from case discussions and role playing to games that simulate analytical or decision-making situations.

Learn from experience. Even here, however, don't learn passively. Think strategically about how you will gain the experience you need. Here are some ways to gain real leadership experience:

- Ask to be assigned to challenging projects that will provide new and unusual problems to solve, such as joining a cross-functional team or a team working on a merger or acquisition.

- Stay alert. Try to observe situations from different perspectives. Watch how different people approach and solve similar problems.

- Don't be afraid to fail. You probably learn more from failing once or twice than from succeeding all the time. The important thing is to take responsibility for your failure and recognize how you could do better the next time.

- Get involved in a variety of assignments; don't just do the same old tasks over and over again.

- Ask for feedback. Find out from others how you are doing. Be open to helpful criticism.

- Elect to join job rotation programs. These programs can help you develop your managerial, technical, business, and communication skills in diverse roles.

Find a true mentor. Mentoring may seem like an excellent source for gaining knowledge about leadership, but the results have been mixed. The mentor should have the experience you want to gain, a genuine willingness to help you along, and a positive relationship with you.

Learn to adapt to different leadership styles

The key to getting the most from all these leadership learning activities is to coordinate them. Know what knowledge, skills, and experiences you need, and plan how to acquire them in an integrated fashion.

What Would YOU Do?

The Prince and the Pauper

AS HIS TAILOR PINNED THE cuff of his new pants, Joseph speculated that Tariq must have some special "in." You'd never know that the two of them had been promoted at the same time. What a difference! Tariq had lunches sent in while he ran meetings in the executive conference room. He chatted up division heads in their offices and strolled the halls with the top people from other departments. Joseph worked like a horse, crunching budgets, making Gantt charts, running team meetings, and hiring new staff. But none of his hard work was bringing him any recognition. The meeting this morning was humiliating. Every time Tariq made a point, everyone nodded in agreement. When Joseph talked, they asked him a lot of questions, as if they didn't quite trust him. Joseph looked in the mirror and wondered if wearing suits like Tariq's would be enough . . . or was there something else he ought to be doing?

Leadership styles are behavioral adaptations to particular situations. Effective leaders learn, practice, and master each of the six leadership styles. Even though these leadership styles are presented as distinct behaviors, they often overlap as needed.

Leadership Styles

STYLE	CHARACTERISTICS	WHEN USEFUL	WEAKNESSES
Coercive	Leader gives orders and expects to be obeyed.	Turnaround situations Natural or manmade disasters Dealing with difficult or problem employees	Inhibits organization's flexibility Weakens employee motivation
Authoritative	Leader establishes overall goal and pushes people to follow.	Business is adrift and needs direction. Business is in a downturn.	Leader's goal may not be the best one. Experts may disagree with the leader.
Affiliative	Leader assumes a "people come first" attitude.	Need to build team cohesion Need to raise low morale	May allow poor employee performance to continue unchecked Employees may not have a sense of direction.
Democratic	Leader gives employees role in decision making.	Need to build organizational flexibility and responsibility	May result in indecision and a sense of confusion
Pacesetting	Leader sets high performance standards.	Highly motivated employees can work on their own.	May feel overwhelming for employees who cannot attain the high standards Some employees may feel resentful.
Coaching	Leader focuses on personal development.	Employees want to change and improve professionally.	Not successful when employees are resistant to change.

You may find some styles more comfortable than others, but the more you can develop a range of styles, the more effectively you will perform as a leader.

Tip: Adapt your leadership style to the needs of your people. Give latitude to those who can handle delegation; provide coaching to those whose skills and confidence need a boost; give explicit directions to those who need close supervision.

What You COULD Do.

Remember Joseph's dilemma?

Is there something else Joseph should be doing? Yes. He needs to figure out what he really wants. There is a difference between being a manager and being a leader. Managers execute and get things done. Leaders determine what needs to be done. Both are valuable, and anyone can do either or both. But Joseph needs to decide which one he will be.

Joseph should not be fooled by appearances. Tariq may be

playing the political game, not the leadership game. In the short term, he may get away with it. In the long term, it will catch him if he is not producing results. Let's assume Tariq is playing the leadership game. He is spending his time working with others to set direction, focusing people and resources on that direction, and worrying about how to build the coalition and energy to get the vision implemented. If that is the case, it is no wonder people are listening to him and involving him in important meetings.

Joseph is spending his time crunching the numbers, preparing the reports, and hiring new staff, all to accomplish the objectives others have set. He is performing technical and managerial work. Both are very valuable, and he may be best suited and happiest performing that type of work. But he should not make the mistake of assuming that working hard and producing results with a managerial focus will qualify him to be a leader. Leaders have a different set of skills. These skills can be developed, but they take constant focus and work.

How to
Craft a Vision

A vision is a mind-picture of your hoped-for end result: what it will look like, how it will function, what it will produce, and how things will be changed by it. A simple, clear, and enduring vision of a better future is a leader's most important motivational tool; you'll refer to it time and again, explaining its benefits and relevance to various audiences as you work to keep them on board. The result of broad-based strategic thinking about the company's most key constituencies and a willingness to take calculated risks, a vision doesn't need to be brilliant or innovative. In fact, some of the best can seem mundane.

Where does your vision fit into the organizational scheme?

In the professional world, the word *vision* has been confused with other important concepts, such as *mission statement*, *strategic objective*, or *slogans*. But a vision, though related to these other concepts, overarches them and gives them meaning.

What comprises a clearly stated, empowering vision?

A vision provides a clear picture of a better future. It offers trust, faith, and hope for everyone in the organization. It becomes a guide for an organization to move from past beliefs, activities, and goals to a future path more suited to the changing needs of the organization and the demands of the economic environment.

A vision should be

- simple and idealistic. It should appeal to core values of the organization.

- challenging but realistic. It's fine for the vision to have lofty language—you want it to be large enough to touch people's core needs for achievement, recognition, and a sense of belonging. But the lofty language has to be easily translated into a realistic competitive strategy. The goals can be aggressive, but they must also be achievable.

- focused. It should serve as a guide in decision making

- beneficial for the organization's stakeholders—customers, stockholders, and employees. It should clearly define the benefits to these various constituencies.

- easy to explain and understand. Even if *implementing* the vision is a complicated process, explaining it should be simple. People won't support what they can't understand.

"When the road ahead is unclear, vision can take you only so far."
—Loren Gary, editor

Develop your vision

You may have a general notion of where you would like your organization to go, but to craft a vision, take the following steps to ensure as much buy-in from stakeholders as possible.

What Would YOU Do?

Great Expectations

WHEN JESSICA TOOK OVER THE DEPARTMENT, she knew that her job was to take it right into the twenty-first century. So she was frustrated with Mary, her mentor and boss, for not giving her the support she needed. They had just finished discussing the new direction for the department for the fourth time. Jessica was starting to feel that Mary was holding out on her. "Where do you see the department going?" she would ask, and Mary would turn the question right back around. "Where do *you* see your department going?" she'd reply. Sometimes she'd make a vague suggestion or offer an encouraging remark, but that wasn't what Jessica was looking for. Why wouldn't Mary tell her what she was supposed to be doing? After all, Mary was the boss! She was supposed to be the one with the grand vision, wasn't she?

Consider first the shared values and ideals of the organization. You won't get very far if you don't adhere to the basic beliefs of the group. Retain whatever is still useful and valuable from the former vision and mission. You don't always have to throw out the entire past to move forward.

A *vision* not only captures *what* the organization does but it expresses *why* the organization exists. A *vision* breathes life into a mission statement. It communicates an image of what can be achieved and why it is a good thing to achieve.

The Central Artery Tunnel Project (Big Dig) is the largest, most complex, and technologically challenging highway project ever attempted in American history. The project will dramatically reduce traffic congestion and improve mobility in one of America's oldest and most congested cities, improve the environment, and lay the groundwork for continued economic growth for millions of New Englanders in the coming new century.

A *mission statement* describes the purpose of the organization by articulating what it does.

To resolve the major traffic problems and endangered quality of life in Boston and New England, we will replace the elevated highway with an underground highway and extend I-90 through a tunnel to Logan Airport.

A *strategic objective* is a near-term tangible outcome, not an enduring reason for being.

The I-90 connector from the MassPike extension to the Ted Williams Tunnel will be completed by January 20, 2003.

A *slogan* is a quick summary.

The Big Dig: Worth the Wait.

"A Buddhist monk once said, 'When you wash dishes, wash dishes.' At first the monk's zen-like thought seemed obvious to me, of no particular value, but upon reflection it began to make more sense. Eventually, I translated it into a phrase that had great significance: 'When in charge, be in charge.' And being in charge means that you must create the future."

— Gordon Sullivan, Chief of Staff, U.S. Army (retired)

Discuss your ideas with various stakeholders. Talk to your superiors and subordinates, and use lateral networking to get valuable information, input, and early support across various functions and departments. Find out what they want and need, and, most importantly, how they react to your vision.

Make sure that all perspectives are represented. Failure to listen to a powerful group or voice can result in problems later on. For example, certain stakeholders may be unwilling to support you at a critical juncture. If you don't incorporate the opinion of an important group, your vision may not address all relevant organizational needs.

Use the results of your research wisely. Incorporate what you learned to define a vision that is both realistic and focused. An effective vision is achievable. Even if it is ambitious, you, your team, and your stakeholders need to be imagining the same set of outcomes.

Ask your team to provide reality checks to help clarify the vision. Listen to those closest to you. Remain flexible. You may have to keep reassessing and revising your vision until it's right.

Clearly define the vision's benefits to all involved. Determine the benefits not only to your unit, but to the broader organization—employees, stockholders, and customers alike. If these stakeholders know "what's in it for me," they'll be more likely to embrace the vision and offer assistance when asked.

Think in terms of satisfying deep human needs. People want to achieve; they want to feel that they belong; they want to have self-esteem and a feeling of control over their lives. If your vision helps to satisfy these needs, you will have plenty of support.

What You COULD Do.

Remember Jessica's dilemma?

There is a difference between boss-ship and leadership. The boss is the one who holds the organization accountable for accomplishing the organization's objectives. The leader, on the other hand, is the one who influences others to accomplish a common goal. Often in organizations today, the boss will not be able to be clear about goals; after all, the environment is changing too fast.

Jessica probably knows more about her job than her boss does. She should set the vision herself, check it out with her boss, and get on with it. Of course she will make mistakes, but she will learn as she goes and make necessary adjustments. The biggest mistake Jessica can make is waiting for the boss to tell her what her objectives should be. She needs to figure out where her department is going, get buy-in from her boss, and keep her informed of the progress she is making; by doing this, Jessica becomes the leader.

Jessica might ask herself: "If I were to go to one of my direct reports, do you think he would say, 'We are very clear where we are going and what we are supposed to accomplish'? Or would his response be, 'Why won't Jessica just tell us what we are supposed to be doing'?" Would your direct reports be clear about what you want from them? Are you a leader or a follower?

Worksheet for Crafting and Maintaining Your Vision

*Complete this worksheet to create a "picture" of your hoped-for vision: what it will look
like, how it will function, what it will produce. Use the results to maintain a record
of your vision and help sell it to others.*

1. Gather Information for the Vision

Write a general description of the hoped-for end result.
I want to expand my successful product into a product line and a recognized
brand name.

What information is necessary to define the vision in detail?
I need to survey current customers to see what additional features or varia-
tions they would be interested in purchasing.

**Who across the organization can provide information, input, and early sup-
port? What do you need to ask them?**
My department head has to agree to this expansion. I need information and
cooperation from marketing and sales.

Input and ideas:
I will meet with the head of the new products department. I'll also ask colleagues from other companies what they think of my ideas.

Who might oppose this effort? What questions do you need to ask them?
Other product managers who have unsuccessful products. I will ask them to
share ideas and perhaps include some version of their products.

The finance VP might not approve the extra resources needed. I'll ask him what
kind of pro forma she needs to approve the plan.

Feedback:
I need feedback from customers and colleagues. Sales team has a good sense
of the market, so I'll ask them for feedback.

2. Craft the Vision

Articulate the vision.
My product line will become a familiar brand for consumers who expect the
best and get it from us. My products will satisfy the customers and increase
in sales and profitability each fiscal year.

(continued)

2. Craft the Vision, *continued*

What is your overall strategy to reach the vision?
Once I have done my homework and collected all the data possible, I will present the business plan to the executive committee.

If they agree to the full expansion, I'll start immediately with designing the line extensions.

3. Checklist: Is Your Vision Realistic?	Yes	No
1. Have team members contributed to the vision and given "buy-in"?	✓	
2. Is the vision realistic and achievable?	✓	
3. Does the end-result of the vision serve the interests of the company's most important stakeholders?	✓	
4. Does the vision include a clear definition of the benefits to all the constituencies that might be affected?	✓	
5. Is the language used in the vision documentation easy to explain and understand?	✓	
6. Does the description of the vision include and articulate a wide range of perspectives (of all affected stakeholders)?	✓	
*If you answer **"no"** to any question, revisit the vision and adjust it to include that aspect.*		

How to Motivate the People You Need

T o ensure that your vision is embraced and fulfilled, you have to pay attention to the people around you—those who will help and those who may hinder your progress. Take care to handle both the political and the personal sides of leading and implementing your vision.

Watch the political scene closely

What do you need to be aware of within your organization? Any leader who wants to make major changes pays attention to her surroundings, understands the changing politics of her world, and marks the realignments that may take place.

Know who could hinder you or help you. Take the time necessary to identify those who might resist you in some way—for example, by blocking your access to needed resources. Plan how you will deal with such problems. Work to win over those key people who aren't enthusiastically behind you or who for some reason may feel threatened by you and your vision.

Build a broad coalition within the organization and among the stakeholders. An effective leader has to be a persuasive communicator. Building coalitions is when this skill becomes particularly useful. You will need cooperation from people at all levels of your organization and beyond (for example, suppliers, contractors, clients, etc.).

Choose carefully whom you assign to important roles. People in key positions need to be competent in their roles and loyal to your vision.

Do something dramatic or bold to shake things up. If the changes you are making are significant, then make sure everyone is involved and understands what's happening. If you are realigning the company's organizational structure, for example, do it quickly and fairly.

Or, if necessary, take tiny steps at first. You may not be able to make dramatic changes simultaneously. There may be technical or political barriers. But even if you can make only small changes that show success, you'll be on your way. Any movement toward your vision should be noted as positive.

Tip: Protect those who voice dissent within the group—they are often sources of new and better ideas for getting the job done.

Care for your people

The people within your own group—whether that group is a company, department, or team—are critical for achieving your vision. Motivating them, caring for them, and leading them is your primary duty.

What Would YOU Do?

War and Peace

HANNAH WAS A PEACEFUL PERSON, and she was ready to call a truce to end the war being waged in her department. Every time she asked her people to agree on a direction, it seemed they understood this as a signal to attack. One group would come up with a plan, and the other would knock it down. Someone else would hurl out another idea, and then everyone would ride roughshod over that. Reaching agreement over what to do was only a preliminary skirmish. Then a "take-no-prisoners" battle would ensue over the means of getting there. By the time her troops finally reached an agreement, Hannah was exhausted. They, on the other hand, seemed energized and ready to move on to the next issue. How could she put a stop to this combat? She considered setting a time limit on the discussions. Or taking sides. Or making the decisions herself. After all, there couldn't be any value to such excruciating conflicts, could there?

Make sure they are with you. Once you are certain your people understand the vision, the mission, and the steps to be taken en route, create a sense of urgency about your shared endeavors. Keep your people excited about what they're doing.

Be prepared for resistance to change. Most people dislike change, even when they know the change is for the better. Rather than ignore that fear of change, recognize and deal with it openly.

Acknowledge and celebrate successes. And continue to celebrate successes, right up to the end. Celebrations can be large and small. A cheer for all, a lunch or picnic, t-shirts or caps—anything to keep spirits up.

Keep people informed. People don't like feeling excluded from the news of progress or of problems. By keeping your people updated, they will be ready to help solve problems as they arise.

Remain committed to the vision. Your commitment will be a model for everyone in the group. If they see you working hard to attain the goals, they will join you.

Empower your people to develop their own leadership skills. The benefits of supporting and trusting others can be enormous. You will gain loyalty as well as experienced and productive employees.

Create a trusting environment

A work environment based on trust allows the individuals of a group to become a cohesive team, working toward the vision for the benefit of all. To achieve this kind of environment,

- Treat everyone, at every level of the hierarchy, with respect and consideration.

- Give everyone's ideas serious consideration.

- Be fair, kind, and courteous at all times.

- Never put other people down.

- Be honest. Admit it when you make a mistake or when you don't have the answer.

- Protect your group. Define a boundary around your group and shelter them from interference. Go to bat for your team to get the resources you need. Show courage in sticking up for your people.

- Do not tolerate scapegoating or misapplied blame.

- Use every reasonable opportunity to foster others' professional growth.

The value of creating this atmosphere is worth the extra effort it may entail because it can

- reinforce trust among team members

- bring people together so they can focus on issues

- help you regulate the friction that is often necessary to do the job

- uphold principles of mutual respect and consideration

- focus on behavior, not personality

- give workers a sense of purpose

- create opportunities for others' professional growth

- foster a positive attitude

- protect a team's members

The result will be that your people will trust and believe you. Credibility is imperative if you are to lead people and achieve your vision.

"You can't believe how many times I'd be sitting home replaying a game I had just played. I'd watch myself come off a pick, and I'd see Danny Ainge, wide open in the corner, and I'd say to myself, "Geez, how did I miss him?" Then I'd go in the next day and say to Danny, "Hey, you were wide open on that play last night in the third quarter. My fault. Call for me next time, and I'll get you the ball."
—Larry Bird, basketball player and coach

Adapt your leadership style to the needs of your people

The members of your group will have different capabilities, needs, and growth potential. Stay flexible in dealing with them; try to respond to them in ways that address their particular needs and interests.

- Be direct with people who are just learning a new skill. They need very specific instructions and ongoing feedback.

- Support people who are learning skills but are still gaining experience. They need direction, but also the freedom to make some mistakes and encouragement to keep going.

- Encourage people who may be highly competent, but who may lack self-confidence. Use positive reinforcement to help them recognize their developing abilities.

- Delegate to highly motivated and experienced people. Don't just delegate work that you find unpleasant. Determine whose expertise or personal experience is suited to a "stretch" assignment, then give that person the freedom and support she needs to succeed.

LEADING AND MOTIVATING TOOLS

Establishing Credibility

Use this checklist to evaluate how well you are able to establish credibility and to create a prodcutive working environment.

Checklist for Establishing Credibility	Yes	No
1. Do you have, and can you demonstrate competence in a particular area?	✓	
2. Do you demonstrate your willingness to work hard on a day-to-day basis?	✓	
3. Do you use whatever power and influence you have to benefit others?	✓	
4. Do you consciously treat everyone with whom you come in contact consistently and fairly?		✓
5. Do you focus on practicing active listening on a day-to-day basis?		✓
6. Do you keep track of and deliver on all promises you make?		✓
7. Do you consistently meet deadlines?		✓
8. Do you remain calm under pressure?		✓

Checklist for Establishing Credibility	Yes	No
9. Do you prepare thoroughly for meetings and presentations?		✓
10. Do you answer all phone calls and respond to all e-mails promptly?	✓	
11. Do you keep accurate and detailed records of projects and activities?	✓	
12. Would colleagues at any level say they have never heard you put another person down?	✓	
13. Do you show that you will not tolerate "scapegoating," or misapplied blame?	✓	
14. Do you listen fairly, kindly and with courtesy to the opinions of others?		✓
15. Do you respect other people's ideas and give each one the same amount of consideration, regardless of level?		✓
16. Do you go to bat for your team to get the resources you need?	✓	
17. Do you shelter your team from interference and show courage in sticking up for your people?	✓	
18. Do you protect voices of dissent, and leaders who are working without authority?	✓	
19. Do you admit it when you make a mistake or when you don't have the answer?	✓	
20. Do you use every reasonable opportunity to foster other's professional growth?	✓	

*If you answer **"yes"** to most of these questions, you are probably doing a good job of establishing your credibility and building a productive work environment.*

*If you answer **"no"** to any questions, you may want to focus on how to improve your performance in that area. Identify how to change your behavior and practice it until it becomes second nature.*

What You COULD Do.

Remember Hannah's dilemma?

Individuals have to decide the style of leadership they prefer. Then they have to decide how to vary their style based on the situation they face. Sometimes you try to change the situation; sometimes you try to change your style. Either can be effective. Hannah has decisions to make. Does she want the group to learn how to solve their own conflicts? Does she want to be more authoritarian and drive the decisions herself? Is the situation such that she needs to make decisions quickly? How will she get buy-in on the decisions that are made?

What Hannah cannot do is let the situation continue as it is. If she wants her group to learn how to work together better, she will have to get in there and help them understand how to resolve conflicts and solve problems. She may have to reorganize the groups. Or she could change the reward systems so they succeed most when everyone succeeds. If she needs decisions made quickly, she may need to become more aggressive about managing input and make the decisions herself. Leadership is about choices. Hannah has to choose what style fits her best and what style best fits the situation.

Keeping Staff and Allies Motivated

Complete this worksheet regularly to track how motivated staff and allies are and to consider how well you are using available strategies to keep them motivated.

Date: January 20

Staff morale is down *(Up? Down? Flat? Mixed?)* **because** the post-holiday slump has hurt our numbers.

Successes or major milestones we have achieved so far:

1. We launched the improved, top-of-the line product. Reception has been slow but positive.

2. We've regrouped the staff so that people with experience in the area are represented on each team.

3. The third tier, lower cost product is in the testing stage, two weeks ahead of schedule.

Individuals who have been instrumental in success to date and what motivates them:

Sian has been creative and enthusiastic. She just believes in the whole project. Martin works hard and produces, but he's too concerned about his status within the group. Marta has been terrific as a source of outside support. She seems to enjoy helping, but she's also networking.

Reward ideas for group:

We need a morale booster. The plan is to provide breakfast every Friday during February. They might even have more energy if they start the day eating instead of dashing about.

Aspects of the "big picture" to emphasize at this point in the effort:

Need to plan a group meeting to celebrate how quickly we're moving along in product development. That should encourage those folks in marketing and sales who haven't seen the payback yet.

(continued)

Checklist: How Well Are You Maintaining Motivation?	Yes	No
1. Have you offered feedback and recognition to individuals who have been instrumental in successes to date?	✓	
2. Have you reported to the team and allies about successes achieved so far and how they relate to the big picture?		✓
3. Have you celebrated successes and the accomplishment of major milestones?		✓
4. Have you spoken recently about the team's ability to overcome problems?	✓	
5. Have you spoken to team members about the importance of their work and how it relates to the company's or unit's larger goals?	✓	
6. Have you remembered to offer special rewards, such as food at team meetings or achievement awards?	✓	
If you answer "no" to any question, consider adjusting your leadership strategies.		

How to Care
for Yourself

Leadership is principally concerned with key tasks and perspectives—but it also has its personal side. Neglect yourself and your own needs, and you'll soon be overwhelmed by the pressures that build on those in leadership positions.

How can you care for yourself?

There are several things—small and large—you can do to avoid the darker side of leadership—the stress that often accompanies the role. The fact that you are succeeding in your career and that your leadership and vision are bringing benefits to the organization should ease your mind. Nevertheless, be wise and try these stress-relieving tactics

- Talk regularly with a confidant—for example, a spouse or trusted friend—about your chief concerns at work.

- If you don't have a mentor, get one. You should be mentored by at least one relatively senior and influential guiding light who is invested in your development and success, and whose advice you can trust without hesitation.

- Take advantage of professional development seminars that help you refine your leadership skills.

- Find a sanctuary, a place you can go to at regular intervals that affords you "a view from the balcony": the chance to reflect on overarching patterns and issues in your work life.

- Don't take things personally if someone criticizes you. As the leader, you're often the lightning rod for other issues.

- Practice relaxation techniques such as deep breathing, taking a short walk, or stretching your body.

- Don't forget to exercise regularly—it relieves stress, helps you sleep better, and gives you more energy.

Tip: Acknowledge the stress you feel.
The burdens of leadership can be daunting.

And remember: Delegation is not a sign of weakness. It makes you a better leader, develops the potential of your staff, and helps you avoid burnout. So, go ahead, shed some tasks. Delegate to subordinates whatever responsibilities you can, but don't pass off just the tedious tasks. Once you've delegated a task, make sure not to let it get pushed back up to you.

Tip: Keep telling yourself that what you
are doing is valuable.

Managing Crises

What Is a Crisis?

A CRISIS IS A CHANGE—sudden or evolving—that results in an urgent problem that must be addressed immediately. A crisis can occur in many forms:

- Life-threatening product defects are discovered.

- Computer hackers shut down a company's entire system and deny access to customers.

- A hard freeze destroys a region's citrus crops.

- A terrorist attack destroys lives and property.

- A key manager dies with no immediate replacement.

Crises are *not* the normal ups and downs of a business cycle—those recurring problems faced in the course of taking risks and exploring new avenues of opportunities. Instead, crises are wrenching, painful events. Yet some good can come out of these difficult experiences. The learning that comes from dealing with a crisis contains the seeds for future success in crisis prevention, crisis management, and, in some cases, even new opportunities.

In this section, you'll learn more about four types of crises: natural or company-related events, technology breakdowns, economic and market forces, and business-relationship crises.

"A crisis is an event that can affect or destroy an entire organization."
—Ian Mitroff

Natural or company-related events

Two types of crises fall in the category of natural or company-related events: uncontrollable natural events and health and environmental disasters related to a company.

An *uncontrollable natural event* of catastrophic magnitude can strike unexpectedly. This event may take the form of an earthquake, typhoon, tornado, hurricane, blizzard, flood, fire, or some other natural disaster that crushes buildings, destroys infrastructures, and interrupts communications.

A *health and environmental disaster related to a company* is a disastrous event that, though not necessarily *caused* by a company, is directly related to the company. The company is either responsible or perceived to be responsible for dealing with it. For example:

- An outside tampers with your company's product in a way that not only harms consumers but also damages the overall image of your product and company.

- Serious product problems come to light, such as defective tires or food contamination, for which your company does bear responsibility.

- Catastrophic accidents, such as major oil spills or radiation leakage, occur on your company's watch.

- Environmental pollution is unknowingly caused by your company in years past. For example, toxic waste with long-lasting harmful effects on wildlife and human health has been dumped into waterways.

What Would YOU Do?

What, Me Worry?

C AL IS THE MANAGER for a successful chain of retail stores. Over the past year, business has been booming. Earnings are up, and profit margins are growing. Because business has been so positive, Cal was surprised when he received a memo from the company's vice president asking him to perform a crisis audit. What did the vice president mean by a *crisis audit*? And why did Cal have to worry about a crisis when business was going so well? Cal didn't have a clue where to begin.

What would YOU do? See *What You COULD Do*.

Technology breakdowns

Everyone knows what it's like when a company's server goes down. In this information age, we are extraordinarily dependent on technology to communicate, store information, do research, buy, and sell. Business today could not function without technology. Here are some common technological problems that could turn into crises:

- **Data loss.** Most companies in the United States do not have data backup plans. According to a University of Texas study, only 6 percent of companies that undergo major data loss will survive that crisis.

- **Security breaches.** A 2001 survey run by the Federal Bureau of Investigation and the Computer Security Institute revealed that 85 percent of large companies and government agencies have detected computer breaches in the past year. Moreover, while most computer attacks come from outside, attacks from inside cause the greatest financial loss.

- **Communications technology.** A retailer's Web site goes offline during the busiest season, stalling orders and frustrating customers and service representatives. A virtual team's Web site goes down, making it impossible for team members to meet a critical deadline. An entire phone system goes out, so that no one in the organization can receive or make calls except on their mobile phones.

- **Outmoded equipment.** When people work on aging equipment or on failing networks, they face a series of ongoing, minor crises every day—inefficient working conditions, difficulty meeting deadlines, lost e-mails, constant frustration. All of these can lead to a major crisis when the systems finally collapse.

Economic and market forces

With a global economy and high-speed information, markets and economies change far more rapidly than they did twenty years ago. These forces can change—or appear to change—quite swiftly. Consider these examples:

- **Market swings.** An unexpected spike or collapse in buying alters predicted sales, product development, and scheduling. Even though regular market swings can make for difficult times, a major disruption in markets results in crises.

- **Trends.** An overall change in consumer demand leaves backward-looking companies in the dust. The rise of the personal computer is an excellent example. Although it was not predicted, it became the new way of life in businesses and homes. Companies that believed that mainframe technology would always be the only market were caught unaware. And many of them went under.

- **Investment bubbles.** Periods of rampant speculation and investment frenzy blow business opportunities out of proportion until the economic realities cause the bubbles to burst. The instant deflation of portfolios, life savings, retirement incomes, and job opportunities creates crises for many.

Tip: Avoid ongoing financial crises by fully funding development projects from the beginning.

Business-relationship crises

All businesses depend on people within the company and outside it, including business partners, vendors, and customers. What does your company do when a crucial leader dies unexpectedly? When a subcontractor in charge of security allows a serious breach at a major airport? When a vendor fails to deliver critical supplies? When an employee is caught embezzling money from a client account? When a partner is indicted? When a major customer goes out of business? When two managers in your company become embroiled in a destructive personal conflict?

Tip: Avoid relationship crises by confronting and negotiating problems before they escalate.

What You COULD Do.

Remember Cal's concern about how to conduct a crisis audit?

Cal might begin by talking with colleagues who work in different areas to better understand what might go wrong in tougher times. If you were responsible for a town dam, you would certainly perform an audit of its structural integrity before a storm caused the water to rise. Likewise, it is important for Cal to perform a crisis audit when things are going well at work so that he can be better prepared should a crisis arise. One of the first steps in performing a crisis audit is to talk with many different people within the organization to gather different perspectives of what could happen. Next, Cal should conduct a *SWOT analysis* to determine the company's *strengths*, *weaknesses*, *opportunities*, and *threats* for each potential crisis.

Six stages of crisis management

All crises—whether related to uncontrollable events, health, technology, changing markets, or business relationships—have the potential to affect your company's reputation, its bottom line, its people, and, ultimately, its ability to do business. Although there is no simple formula for eliminating crises, following the six stages of crisis management can make a big difference in how successfully *your* firm copes with crises.

The stages are as follows:

1. Avoiding the crisis

2. Preparing to manage the crisis

3. Recognizing the crisis

4. Containing the crisis

5. Resolving the crisis

6. Learning from the crisis

In the chapters that follow, we'll examine each of these stages in close detail.

Stage 1: Avoiding the Crisis

CRISES THAT ARE handled poorly often get the greatest media attention. But we don't often hear much about crises that were prevented. Remember the Y2K bug? On New Year's Day, 2000, virtually every computer in the world made the calendar switch to the new millennium without a hitch. All that those who were listening for trouble heard was the quiet sound of a crisis that had been prevented. For years, businesses had worked to solve the Y2K problem before it could strike. And their efforts paid off.

Of course, managers at every level of an organization intercede and prevent minor crises every day. For instance:

- A sales representative notices that a client's name is misspelled on every page of a major sales proposal. The manager has all the copies destroyed, makes the adjustments, and has new proposals printed at an all-night copy center, saving the company from losing a major account.

- A manager foresees a cash flow shortage, takes steps to hurry receivables, and makes sure a credit line is available at the company's bank should the expected cash still not come in.

- A team leader, when informed that a key employee is leaving, takes steps to find a replacement instead of leaving it to the last minute.

All these managers are actively involved in avoiding crises. It's their job. But to practice effective crisis avoidance, you need to take a disciplined approach. And that includes conducting a crisis audit and considering potential crises in the four major areas we discussed earlier.

Conducting a crisis audit

Most managers are already attuned to *possible* and *probable* crises and take some steps to avoid them. But you can become even more effective by preparing for crises when things are going well. The first step is to perform a crisis audit. Look for things that are going wrong now or that have the potential to go wrong in the future.

A crisis audit may look like one more "to do" on your already-long list, but it's an important part of your company's or department's long-term plan.

A crisis audit involves the following steps:

1. **Make crisis planning a part of your strategic planning.** Incorporate the crisis audit into your part of the overall strategic planning process. Whether you run your own business or department, you still have to plan strategically for the future, and that planning needs to include crisis planning.

2. **Get together and share ideas.** People's perspectives about potential crises often differ greatly. No one person has all the information a company needs. By talking to people from other areas of your department, division, or company, you may get some surprising information. Work with colleagues in your department and in other departments to analyze your situation.

3. **Perform a SWOT analysis.** One useful strategic planning tool is the *SWOT analysis* (strengths, weaknesses, opportunities, threats). Conduct the analysis specifically from a crisis perspective. After all, crises often evolve from internal weaknesses or external threats.

   For example, what are your organization's internal weaknesses? Where might a crisis occur in your normal business procedures? For example, are you so understaffed that if one member of the team were to leave, you couldn't function? Or is your infrastructure old and patched together? Are you having quality-control problems that could lead to consumer dissatisfaction or harm?

   And what are your most likely external threats? Which of those threats would be the most damaging to your company? For example, is your competition likely to introduce a radically new product, making yours obsolete?

   Note that many people refuse to recognize the one major threat that looms over the company. By ignoring the reality, any constructive action that might avert or lessen the impact of the problem is left undone. For example, if your company has been successfully producing one major product line, but the managers refuse to acknowledge a new, innovative product that will eventually make your entire product line obsolete, your company very likely will not survive.

4. **Focus on the four major crisis areas.** Consider potential health and environmental disasters, technological breakdowns, economic and market forces, and relationships.

5. **Narrow your crisis-risk list.** In performing the crisis audit, ask yourselves two basic questions: What are the *worst* things that could go wrong? What are the *most likely* or *probable* crises that could occur? You can't possibly address every potential problem or crisis, and some crises simply won't touch your organization. For example, if your company is not located in an earthquake zone, don't put earthquakes on your crisis-risk list. Or if you work at a consulting firm, you won't need to worry about a possible labor strike.

   Narrow your crisis-risk list by focusing on the crises that would have the worst result, would be most likely to occur, and would affect your group or company.

"Make a list of everything that could attract trouble to the business, consider the possible consequences, and estimate the cost of prevention."
   —Norman Augustine

Spotlight on the four major crisis areas

Trying to anticipate every possible type of crisis can be overwhelming. Let's look in more detail at how you focus on the four major crises areas.

- **Health and environmental disasters.** The health and safety of employees, consumers, the general public, and the environment are high priorities. This type of crisis can escalate from a small problem to a major crisis quickly, particularly when people within the institution try to cover it up, place blame, or minimize its importance.

- **Technological breakdowns.** You probably already have a good idea of some of the biggest weaknesses in your company's or department's technology. Maybe it's the phone system, the server, or the Internet connection. Weaknesses in technology can precipitate paralyzing crises if left untreated.

- **Economic and market forces.** Economic forces and market swings can be crises with the greatest opportunities hidden inside—but only if you are prepared. Otherwise, an unexpected market swing can be damaging or even devastating.

- **Relationships.** People are unpredictable. They may do things that you would not think possible, particularly if money or advancement is involved. Organizations with which you have partnered for a long time may also surprise you. Consider, for example, the advertising agency whose *Fortune* 500 client simply closed its doors. Millions of dollars' worth of business was lost. As a manager, you have to deal with numerous and diverse relationships. Look for vulnerable relationships. Be particularly aware of the one vendor, client, or computer whiz whose sudden departure could ruin your company.

Stage 2: Preparing to Manage the Crisis

I N B U S I N E S S , C R E A T I N G a crisis-management plan means making as many decisions as you can before the crisis occurs, so that your energies can go into handling the crisis effectively *if and when it does occur.* Many of these tasks are fairly easy to do when things are going well, but difficult and stressful to do in the middle of a crisis.

However, just as a hospital arranges for a standby generator in case power goes out during surgery, you need backup plans for the set of crises you have identified as the ones your company or department must expect and prepare for.

Recognizing the risks and costs

Consider a major investment company that had only one line of business: helping individual investors buy and sell stocks. When the investment market was at its peak, this company did a booming business. It poured its profits into expanding its business by hiring more people and opening more offices. But when the economy stalled and individual investors stopped buying, the company had no other sources of revenue. The company's stock dropped, and it was forced to make huge layoffs—which affected everyone in the organization. By exploring other sources of revenue and investing some of its profits in those opportunities—and by doing some "what-ifs" about its rate of growth—the company might have lessened some effects of the disaster.

Use the results of your crisis audit as a basis from which to brainstorm potential crises. Question basic assumptions about your business—for both the present and the future. What assumptions do you have that *might* not be true? Ask yourself, "What would happen if people stopped buying our best-selling product?" or "What if demand for our product is so huge that we can't fill our orders?" It's important to do this as a group. Other people can provide a valuable perspective on each other's closely held assumptions. And finally ask, "How would this impact our group?"

Once you've determined what crises you need to plan for, consider ways to minimize these risks. Also, brainstorm the costs for each risk you've identified. Consider everything that might go wrong, and assess the costs if it should. A risk analysis measures more than just costs in terms of money. Determine costs in terms of human health and safety, and other important factors such as ability to meet customers' demands, ability of employees to work and communicate efficiently, and your company's reputation. Prioritize those risks that are most pressing and costly, and deal with them first.

Developing a crisis plan

After you have selected a key what-if scenario and analyzed possible consequences, brainstorm the kinds of decisions that will have to be made. For example, in the event of a natural disaster, employees may have to be evacuated, and second- or third-shift employees might have to be notified. If a problem arises in getting a product to market, additional staff may have to be hired quickly, alternative methods of transportation might have to be lined up, or management may have to answer phones. In the event of an impending strike by transportation workers, you might have to call in a team of employees who drive minivans to bring some people to work, and arrange for some people to work from home.

As you go through this exercise, start to consider who should be making these decisions. Also, perform a reality check on your plan by brainstorming possible unintended—and undesirable—side effects. For example, when a chain of auto-repair shops wanted to boost sagging sales, management offered mechanics sales incentives. The more work they brought in, the bigger bonus they'd make. Unfortunately, some of the mechanics began recommending unnecessary repairs. Customers complained that they were being ripped off, and the chain's reputation suffered. Similarly, a factory offered incentives for every defective product turned in, but it soon turned out that some workers were deliberately damaging products in order to receive the awards. And when a pizza company promised to deliver its "pizza in 30 minutes or it's free," speeding drivers caused car accidents.

You don't have to cover every eventuality, but thinking things through carefully can help prevent such unanticipated problems.

Forming a crisis-management team

The outcome of the crisis depends on the performance of the people making the decisions. The better prepared they are, the

Steps for Developing a Crisis Plan

1. **Identify obstacles and fail points.**

   What factors could make the crisis worse? Lack of staff? No evacuation plan? Technology? Weather? Lack of money? Lack of knowledge? Brainstorm obstacles and fail points, and then determine ways to deal with them.

2. **Create a resource plan.**

   Depending on the type of crisis, consider what you may need to resolve it. Then plan for those resources to be on hand when needed. For example, employees traveling to dangerous parts of the world may need quick access to cash. Determine what resources you need, how you will get them, and who will be in charge.

3. **Create a communication plan.**

   Decide who will need to know about the crisis—include both internal and external people. Then develop a communication plan so that each key person will be informed as needed. The communication plan could be as simple as an emergency contact list or a more complex communication tree designating the flow of messages.

4. **Distribute resource and communication plans.**

   Make sure all key people have and understand the resource and communication plans. Call a meeting to review the plans and go over each person's role during an emergency. A mock crisis drill could even be performed to test whether the plans will actually work.

better the crisis will be handled. Determine who on your team will:

- Be involved in handling each aspect of the crisis
- Make what kinds of decisions
- Notify authorities within the company
- Notify employees, government agencies, media, and so forth
- Decide whether employees should stay home
- Decide to evacuate a building
- Decide to hire temporary personnel in the event of an unexpected business rush

Once these decisions have been made, make sure that every person on the team has a backup in case they are unavailable.

In addition, create and distribute a list of all phone numbers, e-mail addresses, and ways to reach critical team members. Have people put the list on their computers, in their mobile-phone address books, on wireless communicators, and in their home offices . . . wherever anyone on the team could possibly need access to it.

Then, identify both formal and informal networks within the organization. Who are key players you may need to rely on in a crisis?

Creating a communications and resource plan

Create lists of all people who will need to be contacted in the event of a crisis—not just the members of the team—and how to contact them. You may need to include all employees, vendors, and customers.

> Tip: Make it a point to establish relationships that you don't already have. When a crisis comes, it's a lot easier to handle if you already know all the players.

Also, for each crisis on your list, think about what resources will be needed to handle the situation. For example, if you manage a research project in a pharmaceutical firm, you may have to prepare for a biological or health-related crisis. If you are trying to develop a market niche in an underdeveloped country, your employees may be in real physical danger. In both these examples, the resources required would be very different—from a store of specific antidotes to a detailed escape plan.

> Tip: In creating a crisis-communications plan, make a list of the five questions you would least like to be asked regarding the crisis. (Be assured that someone will ask them.) Prepare answers to the questions.

Stage 3: Recognizing the Crisis

THE CHIEF EXECUTIVE officer of a major corporation was alerted one day that the president of one of its subsidiaries—a film company—had been accused of embezzling money and forging checks. But the CEO refused to believe that the film-company president would ever commit such crimes. He ignored the problem, but it didn't go away. By the time the CEO decided to fire the president, the charismatic thief had gotten board members lined up on his side. The board insisted on keeping the president. The situation worsened, with reports coming out in the paper tarnishing the name of the film company, the corporation, and all involved—including the CEO. It was an ugly, painful crisis. And it could have been avoided if the chief had recognized it as a potential crisis and dealt with it promptly.

Like this CEO, many managers don't want to face unpleasant situations. Unfortunately, unpleasant situations can be signs of an impending crisis. Pay attention to that voice inside you that says, "Uh-oh, there's something wrong!" The CEO must have been very disturbed when he found out that his film-company president was accused of embezzling. But he rationalized the event by telling himself that what he had heard was impossible.

Is it a crisis?

On a day-to-day basis, managers learn of many disturbing facts and events. Instead of trying to ignore them, rationalize them, or minimize their importance, turn around and face them. Take a minute to step outside yourself and question the event and its consequences.

First, *characterize the event.* Use the checklist shown in the table "Is it a crisis?" to determine whether you're dealing with an impending crisis.

Second, *evaluate the size of the crisis.* Once you've realized that you are dealing with a crisis, determine its scope and magnitude.

Is it a crisis?

Has the event in question caused, or does it have the potential to cause . . .	Yes	No
Injury to any person?		
A threat to the health or safety of any person?		
A threat to the environment?		
A breakdown in your company's ability to serve customers or a threat to your company's reputation?		
A serious threat to employees' morale and well-being?		
A loss of data?		
Serious financial loss?		
A legal action against your company or an individual associated with it (employee, subcontractor, partner)?		
Interpreting your score: If you answered yes to any of the above questions, you are probably dealing with an impending crisis.		

Quickly gather as much information as you can. Ask yourself questions such as the following:

- How many people are involved? Who are they?
- How long is this likely to last?
- Have any laws been broken? If yes, which ones?
- Who already knows about the crisis? What do they know?
- Who needs to know?
- What are the costs already in terms of health? Money? Reputation?

Third, *self-reflect*. Evaluate how you might manage the situation. Are you someone who tends to underreact? If so, maybe you need to become more concerned. Or do you have a tendency to overreact? If yes, you may need to calm down.

Fourth, *consider your values*. What is important? What is the *right* thing to do? For example, if an employee is breaking the law—and using the company to do it—what is your responsibility? Or if a subcontractor is disposing of toxic waste from your company illegally, harming the environment and possibly endangering lives, and you suspect the company is turning a blind eye to it, what should you do?

If it is a crisis, how will you deal with it?

Suppose you've decided that you do have a crisis on your hands. What do you do? You may have to deal with some aspects of the situation immediately, but you will also need to come up with a flexible plan for dealing with the crisis's short- and long-term effects. The following strategies can help:

- **Get a team in place.** Assemble your crisis-management team as quickly as possible. Depending on the scope of the situation, members of the team may need to be assigned to the crisis full-time. If the crisis is big enough, or of long enough duration, you may need to pull the crisis-management team off some or all of their regular duties. If you have performed a crisis audit, then your team members will already know what their roles are and how to communicate with each other.

- **Get the information you need.** Throughout the crisis, you'll need key information about what's happening—as it happens. You'll need to ask the right people the right questions. Work with your team to make sure the information keeps flowing. You'll also need to make sense out of the information you get. Sort out what's relevant and what isn't, what's important and what's trivial. It's easy to get bogged down in details, so step back every now and then, and take a broad view of the situation.

- **Get a sounding board.** At this phase of the crisis, it's also important to have a sounding board—a person you can trust who will help you talk through ideas, information, and decisions.

Tip: If you've determined that you are facing a crisis, get the facts as quickly as you can, to the best of your ability.

Stage 4: Containing the Crisis

WHEN A CRISIS DOES strike, the first thing you must do is contain it. Your goal is to stop the hemorrhaging fast. You must make decisions quickly. Be on the scene. Your physical presence is important. It lets everyone know that your company cares about what is happening. And you must communicate critical information to key people.

For example, when a supermarket chain was accused by a major TV network of selling spoiled meat, the value of its stock plummeted. But the management team responded quickly. They gathered the facts by not only listening to the news media and hearing the message from stockholders but by paying attention to and working with their own employees as well.

They immediately stopped the practice of selling less-than-fresh meat, and they put large windows in the meat-preparation areas so the pubic could watch meat being packaged. They expanded their employee training, gave public tours of their facilities, and offered consumer discounts to draw people back into the stores. The company eventually earned an excellent rating from the Food and Drug Administration, and its sales returned to normal.

Demonstrating decisiveness and compassion

When a torrential rain flooded a section of a building, the water destroyed computers, carpeting, paper records, and the workspace of ten employees. The manager was on the scene as the workers showed up in the morning, to help them and to direct immediate cleanup efforts. After the cleanup, workers began having breathing problems and headaches. Though the carpet had been cleaned, it was determined that it was probably infested with mold. Instead of trying to clean the carpet again or waiting for budgetary approval, the manager immediately ordered all the carpet in the area to be removed and replaced.

This manager demonstrated two essential qualities necessary in a crisis: decisiveness and compassion. First, his presence on the scene showed that he, and the company, cared. Later, his decisiveness in replacing the toxic carpeting demonstrated that the health of employees was more important than any other consideration.

Decisiveness is not always easy, but it's important when you're containing a crisis. Often, you have to act on too little or inexact information. If there is no workable contingency plan in place, if there are no guidelines for the situation, and if there are no trusted confidants, there is still always your conscience. Ask yourself, "What's the right thing to do?" And then do it, hoping it is the right thing!

Compassion is a part of many organizations' cultures, and it is typically rewarded in those cultures. But not always. Some companies pride themselves on having a ruthless and competitive culture. Nevertheless, a manager still has the power to set the tone for his or her own division. No manager—regardless of the corporate culture—has to abandon compassion or humanity, especially during a crisis.

What Would YOU Do?

Stop That Leak

INDRA MANAGES THE IT department at DatServ, an information services company. One day, a technician from her group comes to her with troubling news: apparently, a hacker has broken into one of DatServ's customer databases and corrupted some of the information in it. Luckily, DatServ's tech staff has quickly reprogrammed the company's security software and recovered the damaged data. The staff has also reassured the affected customer that no permanent harm was done to its database. Indra decides also to review DatServ's security software, with an eye toward making any necessary changes to prevent further hacking.

However, news of the incident has spread throughout the industry. The affected DatServ customer tells other customers about the security breach. Equally alarming, a journalist calls Indra's department, looking for information. Apparently, someone has leaked word of the incident to an industry trade magazine.

Even though DatServ fixed the breach quickly and repaired the damage, it seems Indra now has a public relations disaster on her hands. She's got to say something about the situation to key people—including DatServ's top management, major customers, employees, and the media. But what?

What would YOU do? See *What You COULD Do*.

> **Tip:** While managing a crisis, acknowledge and show sympathy for human suffering.

Communicating about the crisis

Anyone who is handling a crisis is going to have to communicate about it with others. These others could be the general public or your immediate employees, vendors, suppliers, and clients. In any case, you will need to communicate to your direct reports how the crisis will impact them and what they need to do. What you say and how you say it are critical. You are managing the perceptions of people whose reactions can drastically affect what happens. The way you communicate can precipitate actions that can make the crisis worse—or better. A crisis, by definition, means that there is bad news. Dealing with pain and anger early on can forestall far worse problems later on. Your goal is to contain the overall crisis, not to make the present moment easier.

"One's objective should be to get it right, get it quick, get it out, and get it over."
—Warren Buffett

When communicating during a crisis:

- **Expect rumors and false information.** During a crisis, people crave information—whether it's true or not. Use the communication strategy you've developed as part of your crisis planning to address and stop the flood of false news.

- **Notify key people.** Inform anyone who needs to know—company management, customers, employees, suppliers, government authorities—and do so quickly, within two hours, if possible. If you have created a communication plan or list of important phone numbers, now is the time to use it.

- **Stick to the facts.** Whether you're talking to coworkers, authorities, or the media, make your message straightforward and honest. Avoid these typical, but inappropriate messages: "No comment." "We haven't read the complaint." "A mistake was made." Give all the facts that you know. You are not obligated to speculate or to cover up, because lying and speculating will only damage your credibility and your company's credibility if and when you are proved wrong. Moreover, communicate all the bad news at once. It's like pulling off a sticky bandage. It will hurt now, but it will be over soon.

Tip: Record a voice message on a phone line at the end of each day, so that people can call and hear what is really going on. Your voice is a powerful communications tool. Also, use a Web site to gather and post important information. Your company Web site has credibility and is easily accessible by everyone.

What You COULD Do.

Remember Indra's dilemma about what to say to the media (as well as DatServ's management, customers, and employees) about the security breach?

In communicating to these various constituencies about the security breach, Indra should convey all the bad news at the same time (rather than doling it out in small pieces). Moreover, she should tell people everything she knows about what happened. By taking this approach, she comes across as open and honest. Journalists and other stakeholders won't conclude that she's hiding something, and they won't feel compelled to keep digging for more "dirt." Though this approach can be painful—like pulling off a sticky bandage all at once—the pain will end much sooner than if Indra were to omit or cover up key facts.

Additional suggestions for Indra include preparing carefully for any press conference or presentation, being honest about what she knows and doesn't know, and accepting responsibility for handling the crisis (not causing it). She should also avoid promising anything that she can't deliver. (It is wiser to underpromise and then deliver more, than to overpromise and come up short.) Finally, Indra should resist any urge to qualify expressions of sympathy (e.g., "We're sorry this happened, *but* . . .").

Stage 5: Resolving the Crisis

B Y DEFINITION, A crisis requires fast, confident decision making. But how do you make good decisions when events are moving quickly, when things are confusing, and when it's hard to sort out what's important? How can you stay on track? Managing the emotions that accompany a crisis, understanding the leader's role, and taking effective action can help.

Managing the emotions

Typically, three emotions can combine to create stress for everyone experiencing a crisis:

- Fear of disaster

- Anticipation of a potentially positive outcome

- Desire for the crisis to be over

Under stress, you feel the pressure to make a decision. But the pressure can push you to a state of panic where you are making decisions solely to be "doing something." In reality, however, you are dispersing energy and resources—and this energy is your source of strength. Use the power of positive stress to handle the crisis as a confident leader.

Try to avoid "toxic" stress responses. Often, people respond to these natural and conflicting feelings of fear, hope, and despair in ways that can aggravate—rather than relieve—the crisis. Consider these examples of common ineffective and often harmful responses:

- **When in doubt, scream and shout.** Making noise may give you the feeling that you're doing something, but it wastes energy and won't resolve the crisis.

- **Hide your head in the sand.** At times, the pressure to act becomes so stressful that a manager slips into a state of paralysis and can't make any decisions at all.

TOXIC STRESS RESPONSE *n* **1:** a response to the emotions triggered by a crisis that aggravates rather than relieves the crisis

---

How to handle your uncertainty and fear during a crisis? Use the energy you derive from these emotions to face the crisis and deal with it as effectively as possible. In addition, adapt your response according to whether the crisis is sudden or long-running. For example, if the crisis flares up and is over quickly, then try these simple steps to maintain your emotional balance.

1. **Stop.** As soon as you begin to feel the first rush of anxiety flooding your mind, say "Stop!" to yourself. To face a crisis, you need to have a clear mind as unclouded by anxiety, toxic stress, and fear as possible. Thus, recognizing those feelings and verbally pushing back can block them from controlling your mind and actions.

2. **Breathe.** Take a deep breath. Just as the word *stop* blocks the negative thoughts from your mind, breathing overcomes the stress-induced tendency to hold your breath.

3. **Reflect.** By interrupting the pattern of toxic stress and giving yourself energy through breathing, you can now focus on the *real* problem: the crisis you face. By reflecting on your stress response, you can begin to distinguish the different levels of thought and to sort out reasonable from irrational stress responses. You can see the practical situation more calmly and realistically and distinguish it from the distortions of your anxiety-influenced thoughts.

4. **Choose.** With your attention now on the practical situation itself, you can choose to find real solutions, follow the crisis plan your group has developed, and tend to the needs of the people you lead.

Some crises start as a slow burn and then break out into a wildfire of trouble. For example, financial crises often begin as small problems in a company's receivables or perhaps cash flow fluctuations. Then they build to an inability to borrow or cover basic expenses. You may have a sense of the emerging crisis for several weeks or months, yet you're unable to stop the spread of trouble.

During this kind of crisis, when you're coping with stress over long periods of time, taking care of yourself becomes even more important. Long-term stress can be toxic—physically harmful to you. Taking care of yourself gives you the strength and stamina to take care of the impact of the crisis. So even when you feel hemmed in by the growing crisis, remember to:

- Talk to people—don't become isolated

- Get enough sleep

- Exercise regularly

- Eat a balanced diet

- Avoid alcohol, caffeine, and sugar

- Take a break whenever you can

- Find humor wherever you can

Understanding the leader's role

Whether as the CEO of a large corporation or a supervisor of a department, an effective leader finds out as quickly as possible what the real problem is during a crisis. Often, there will be a flurry of information, most of it inaccurate. It's your task to discover the truth and face it by asking the right people, listening to the most reliable voices, and going to the right places.

A leader in a crisis responds by:

- **Facing the crisis**—turning fear into positive action

- **Being vigilant**—watching for new developments and recognizing the importance of new information

- **Maintaining focus on the priorities**—ensuring that people are safe first, and then assessing the next most critical needs

- **Assessing and responding** to what is in his or her control and ignoring what is not

Taking action

As a leader, you take action on several fronts to resolve the crisis:

- **Activate your crisis plan.** Once you understand the problem, there are probably only a few realistic options open to you. If you have a crisis plan in place, use it.

- **Help everyone work together.** A leader has the power to draw people together to act as a team. If your people know you are in charge, they will respond to your direction.

- **Avoid blaming others.** As the crisis heats up, the impulse to blame people can become irresistible. Certainly, a team member's incompetence or serious error may have caused the crisis, or it may be perpetuating it. However, during the heat of the crisis, trying to find a scapegoat is counterproductive. Focus your people on handling the crisis, not on blaming others. Later, after the crisis, it will be up to you to analyze whether a person should be reprimanded in some way. However, keep in mind that constant faultfinding lowers morale and stifles the creativity and commitment you need to solve the problem. Create an atmosphere where people look forward to what needs to be done, not backward to who was at fault.

- **Do what needs to get done.** Rules, policies, structures, procedures, and budgets are created to maintain order and provide a productive process in the normal course of business. However, most rules were not created with a crisis in mind. Do whatever has to be done, and don't worry about the "rules."

Consider this example of how a leader took effective action during a crisis. When a catalog retailer that offered a large number of custom products—monogrammed bags, sweaters, and so forth—put out its holiday catalog, it was shocked by the positive response. From the moment the catalog was released in October, the company's phone lines were swamped. The retailer hired temporary help to work the phones, but still had a tremendous bottleneck: customizing and shipping the products. It was the holiday season. The head of distribution recognized that if they didn't get everything shipped in time for the holidays, there might not be a next season.

So the CEO put out a call for help and recruited management and administrative staff to work in the warehouse in the evenings—after they had done their regular jobs. Everyone worked together for six long and grueling weeks—everyone from the top down. By working as a team, the whole company eventually enjoyed astonishing success by growing 80 percent in that one year. What could have been a crisis and failure was turned around by teamwork.

Tip: Determine who can help you handle the crisis, and bring them together immediately. You may need to create a team whose job it is to handle the crisis, while others in your department or business are charged with running business as usual.

Stage 6: Learning from the Crisis

WHEN YOU SURVIVE a crisis, don't just try to put it behind you. Rather, take the opportunity to learn from the experience and make changes to avoid or prepare for another similar event. Engineers, for instance, use earthquakes as a learning experience to plan for stronger roads, bridges, and buildings. They use massive floods to determine the best ways for people to adapt to the power of nature (build dams or dikes) or yield to that power (move out of a flood plain).

You, too, can do a postcrisis audit to learn and even profit from the event. For example, when everyone in the catalog company worked overtime to fill a large volume of orders they hadn't expected to receive, they successfully handled the immediate crisis. But operating in crisis mode is an ineffective way to work all the time. It takes its toll on morale, turnover, and the health of everyone, especially the manager. After the rush at the catalog company, people were given large bonuses and extra vacation time. Then management took steps to plan for the next year, so the company would be prepared to meet a large demand—with less pressure on the employees.

POSTCRISIS AUDIT *n* **1:** a review of what happened during a crisis and how people responded, designed to enable the organization to learn from the event

---

Reviewing how the crisis was handled

Plan the timing of the crisis review soon enough after the event so that people remember details, but long enough afterward for some emotional healing to have taken place. Start by analyzing the crisis from beginning to end. Pinpoint actions, assumptions, and outside factors that precipitated the crisis. Ask yourself the following questions:

- Knowing what we knew then, could we have prevented the crisis? If so, how?

- At what point did we realize we were in a crisis? Could we have recognized the signs earlier?

- What warning signals went off that we may have ignored?

- What warning signals did we pay attention to?

- What were the early signs? Why were they turning points?

- What did we do right? What could we have done better?

- What were the stress points in the system that failed?

Planning for the next one

Knowing what you know now, how can you prevent the same type of crisis from occurring again? Create a plan so that you learn from what you know.

- **Get input from everyone.** You need to get everyone's story, but pay attention in particular to those with expertise in the areas of importance. If the crisis was technological, then listen to the computer experts, the IT group, the network engineers. If the crisis was relational—a critical vendor cuts off your supply of goods—talk to your buyers, but then go out in the field and find out what happened and why.

- **Incorporate the ideas and information in your next round of strategic planning.** You've already performed your first crisis audit. Now you'll have much more knowledge to improve the revised audit and the crisis-prevention plan.

Successful managers make each crisis a learning experience. For example, the catalog company experienced a crisis when its phone lines were swamped after the release of its holiday catalog. Management listened to employees and outside consultants. Consultants analyzed workflow, looking at bottlenecks and technology. And everyone in the company who had worked in the warehouse to help get through the crunch now understood firsthand how the business was run. Their experience had taught everyone a great deal. The CEO set up a system to tap into the cumulative knowledge of the company's workforce. The firm set up a suggestion program and put many resulting ideas into practice. Each quarter, it gave a $100 reward to the employee who came up with the best idea.

Tip: Break the crisis down into component parts, to analyze how you might handle a similar crisis more effectively next time. If you look at the problem as one big tidal wave, you will find it more difficult to learn from the experience.

Tracking results

Track the results of changes you make after the crisis. How are they working? Will they actually reduce the negative impact of a future event? For example, as a result of a comprehensive analysis and much planning, the catalog company was well prepared for the next season. Some of the realizations and improvements that were generated by the analysis included those shown in the table "Tracking results."

Tracking results

Problem identified	Action taken
The outdated IT system was incapable of handling the large volume of business.	The system was redesigned and overhauled. The division grew from one of the smallest in the company to one of the largest.
There were too many colors for customizable items, which caused delays in processing orders.	The number of colors offered was reduced; offerings were streamlined.
Most of the orders came in a three-month period, while it was slow the rest of the year.	More catalogs were offered throughout the year.
Many shoppers ordered at the last minute, creating enormous demand on resources at one time.	To spread out the frequency of demand, incentives were offered to encourage customers to order earlier in the season.
Too many catalogs went out at once.	The release of catalogs and ability to respond was tracked, so that systems were always in place to handle demand.

Making
Decisions

What Is Decision Making?

A S A MANAGER, YOU are faced with decisions every day. Some decisions are straightforward, such as deciding which team member to assign to a specific project. Others are more complex, such as selecting a new vendor or deciding to discontinue a product due to weak sales.

Many managers tend to view decision making as an event—a choice to be made at a single point in time, usually by an individual or a small group. In reality, however, significant decisions are seldom made in the moment by one manager or in one meeting. Simply put, decision making is a social or group process that unfolds over time.

"Effective executives know that decision making has its own systemic process and its own clearly defined elements."
—Peter Drucker

Decision making as a group process

Important decisions, such as changing the strategic direction of a group or hiring a new manager, typically require time and input from many individuals and sources of information throughout an organization. Hence, decision making can more accurately be viewed as a *group process.*

Managers who recognize decision making as a group process increase their likelihood of making more effective decisions. Why? By taking time, they are able to identify and assess the issues associated with making the decision. By involving others, they weigh different perspectives and deepen the discussion. Perhaps most important, taking a process-driven approach is more likely to lead to broader acceptance of the decision—which in turn leads to more effective implementation.

Making decisions: eight steps

We can think of the decision-making process as consisting of eight steps:

1. **Setting the stage.** You select participants and determine the approach you will take to reach a decision: will you aim for consensus or vote by majority? During the meetings, especially the earliest ones, you set the tone for the group by encouraging open dialogue and promoting healthy debate.

2. **Recognizing obstacles.** Certain individual biases and group dynamics can be obstacles in the decision-making process. By predicting and recognizing these tendencies, you can take action to avoid them.

3. **Framing the issue.** A successful decision depends on a clear understanding of the issue at hand and its root cause(s).

4. **Generating alternatives.** After you've clarified the issue, you brainstorm and generate creative conflict to develop alternative courses of action and ways of proceeding.

5. **Evaluating alternatives.** Next, you assess the feasibility, risk, and ethical implications of each possible course of action.

6. **Making a decision.** You choose an alternative.

7. **Communicating the decision.** You decide who should be notified of your decision, and communicate it effectively.

8. **Implementing the decision.** You determine what tasks will be required to put the decision into action, assign resources, and establish deadlines.

Throughout this eight-step process, you also continually assess your decision-making effectiveness and make changes as needed to improve it.

In the sections that follow, we'll take a closer look at each of the eight steps in the decision-making process. Then we'll examine ways to assess the effectiveness of your process.

Step 1: Setting the Stage

S ETTING THE STAGE for the decision-making process is critical to making successful choices. This step consists of:

- Selecting the right people to participate in the process

- Choosing an approach for making the actual decision

- Creating a climate that promotes healthy debate and allows for diverse viewpoints

Let's take a closer look at each of these three tasks.

Determining who will participate in the decision

A group of people with diverse perspectives is more likely to generate a variety of thoughtful ideas about how to make a particular decision than a group of individuals with the same background. When you choose people for your decision-making group, look for individuals who are likely to express differing points of view and who represent different interests. Your group should include:

- **Key stakeholders.** These are the people who will be most directly affected by the decision or who have a stake in the decision. You need their buy-in to put the decision into effect. Since they are more likely to support a decision they helped make, include them early in the process to ensure an efficient implementation.

- **Experts.** Experts can educate the group and provide information about the feasibility of various courses of action you're considering. Keep in mind that you may need more than one area of expertise represented in your group.

- **Opponents.** If you are aware of individuals who may oppose the decision and block its implementation, invite them to one or more of your meetings. Involving potential opponents early on can eliminate obstacles down the road.

Ideally, your group should be small in size, preferably between five and seven members. Depending on the complexity of the decision at hand, you may want to involve as many as ten or as few as two people in the decision-making process.

Selecting a decision-making approach

Once you've selected the participants, determine what decision-making approach you will take. The group you assemble needs to understand up front the process it will follow and how the final decision will be made. The spectrum of group decision-making approaches includes four general types:

- **Consensus.** All team members meet together to discuss the proposal openly and strive to reach agreement, with everyone accepting the final decision.

What Would YOU Do?

Keeping Up with the Joneses

L ESLIE IS A TECHNICAL manager at Smith Enterprises, an industrial-quality tool manufacturing company. The products that she and her engineers develop are manufactured internally. Leslie knows the manufacturing department is overburdened and frequently delivers its products late, resulting in delayed shipments to customers. She's noticed that Smith Enterprises' main competitor—Jones Tool, Inc.—as well as several additional rival firms, is developing products faster by outsourcing the manufacturing process. In light of this, she's afraid that her company will lose new business. Leslie's boss has asked her to investigate outsourcing options and decide how they should proceed. She thinks the answer is clear—manufacturing the products externally would save significant amounts of time and money. Leslie senses that her boss is in favor of this option as well. She is inclined to personally gather the information that supports outsourcing and submit a proposal to her boss immediately but wonders whether that would be the best first step.

What would YOU do? See *What You COULD Do*.

- **Majority.** The group votes and the majority rules. The team leader may elect to break a tie, if necessary.

- **Qualified consensus.** The team tries to reach a collective agreement, but if it is unable to do so, the team agrees that the team leader makes the decision.

- **Directive leadership.** The leader makes the decision and then informs the group of the decision that was made. A crisis or sudden unexpected emergency is a classic example of when this approach might be necessary.

These approaches, with the exception of directive leadership, vary in the extent that they empower the participants and create a sense of responsibility within the group. Be aware, however, that regardless of approach, when a group is trying to find areas of agreement, it may avoid exploring minority viewpoints. Your job as a manager is to encourage exploration of all ideas, no matter what approach you will take to make the decision.

Fostering the right climate

To help your group generate creative solutions to problems and evaluate them critically, choose diverse settings for your meetings. Such settings might include conference rooms that you don't typically work in, off-site locations, or a familiar location with the furniture rearranged to facilitate face-to-face discussion. When people are removed from traditional settings, such as a boardroom or a supervisor's office, they tend to speak more freely because they feel less constrained by office hierarchies.

You'll also need to create a consistent climate, or tone, for your decision-making meetings. The climate you establish strongly influences how members of your team interact with one another.

Consider the following scenario: A manager at a software development company has been charged with assigning limited resources to the firm's current projects. The manager calls a meeting with all of her project leaders to discuss how the resources will be allocated. The discussion quickly turns into an argument. Each project leader advocates for his or her project. The debate gets heated as the conversation goes around in circles, and each project leader disparages the others' efforts. Ultimately, the manager decides to assign the limited resources to three projects. The project leaders leave the meeting exhausted and frustrated.

What went wrong? The manager did not manage the decision-making process effectively, and the meeting deteriorated into an *advocacy* mode. The project leaders viewed the meeting as a competition. They advocated for their positions without considering the needs of other departments or the company as a whole. In advocacy situations, people tend to offer only the information that supports their case and omit details that might weaken it. As a result, the discussion can quickly deteriorate into personal attacks, giving rise to negative emotions.

In a perfect world, decisions would be made using an *inquiry* approach—an open process in which individuals ask probing questions, explore different points of view, and identify a wide range of options with the goal of reaching a decision that the group creates and owns collectively. In an inquiry mode, individuals set aside their personal opinions or preferences in order to arrive at a decision that is best for the group or organization.

The table "Approaches to decision making" illustrates the advocacy approach versus the inquiry approach to decision making.

While inquiry is an ideal, it is seldom met in practice. It is extremely difficult for individuals to discuss ideas or issues without expressing their opinions. A more realistic and effective technique for arriving at a decision is one that *balances* advocacy with inquiry. Group members leave their personal agendas behind and enter the

Approaches to decision making

	Advocacy	Inquiry
Concept of decision making	A contest	Collaborative problem solving
Purpose of discussion	Persuasion and lobbying	Testing and evaluation
Participants' role	Spokespeople	Critical thinkers
Patterns of behavior	• Strive to persuade others • Defend your position • Downplay weaknesses	• Present balanced arguments • Remain open to alternatives • Accept constructive criticism
Minority views	Discouraged or dismissed	Cultivated and valued
The outcome	Winners and losers	Collective ownership

meeting with the intention of acting as unbiased participants. They may advocate for a position they feel strongly about, but they also inquire into other viewpoints and consider alternatives. They understand that the goal is to find the best solution for the group as a whole, even if it means that some individuals in the group might be negatively affected by the decision. Generally, in sessions that balance advocacy with inquiry, people share information freely and consider multiple alternatives.

What You COULD Do.

Remember Leslie's dilemma about how to initially approach the outsourcing decision?

What may seem like a clear answer to Leslie may not be the best approach to arriving at the best business decision. In order for Leslie to make the best decision, she needs to assemble a group that first will concentrate on understanding why Smith Enterprises' current process is costly and inefficient and then will explore possible alternatives for improving the process. The group should consist of engineers as well as people outside her department—for example, someone from manufacturing and possibly sales. Including people with diverse backgrounds and areas of expertise will help Leslie make a more informed decision. Once the team identifies the underlying reasons for the issue they are facing, they should then generate and evaluate a number of alternatives for resolving the issue. Although Leslie's inclination is to solve the problem a certain way, she should look for information and evaluate options that support alternative solutions. By involving others and evaluating a wide range of options, Leslie will increase her chances of making a successful decision.

Step 2: Recognizing Obstacles

ᴅᴇᴄɪsɪᴏɴ ᴍᴀᴋɪɴɢ ɪs made difficult by common, often unconscious, obstacles that frequently inhibit a decision maker's ability to determine the optimal choice. Such obstacles include cognitive biases and unproductive group dynamics. While it is almost impossible to eliminate these obstacles, recognizing them in yourself and in the members of your group will help you make more objective decisions.

Anticipating cognitive biases

Here are some common examples of cognitive biases—distortions or preconceived notions—that people encounter when making decisions.

- **Bias toward the familiar and toward past successes.** We tend to base our decisions on events and information that are familiar to us. For example, Susan, a brand manager, remembers her launch of a new product in Spain three years ago; it was her first big marketing success. She also vaguely remembers that a similar launch strategy was *un*successful in a number of other countries. Because her memories of the successful Spanish launch are so vivid, she emphasizes this experience and discounts the evidence of unsuccessful launches elsewhere. When Susan tries to extend a new brand into Portugal, her efforts fail. While the strategy used for the Spanish launch may have been a good starting point, her reliance on a prior success led to incorrect assumptions about the Portuguese market.

- **Bias toward accepting assumptions at face value.** We are generally overconfident in our assumptions and therefore generate too few alternatives. For instance, Brock purchases a software package offered by the largest vendor without collecting competitive bids. He assumes that because the package works for other users in the same industry, it will work for him. He fails to investigate other software packages that might better meet his needs.

- **Bias toward the status quo.** We have a tendency to resist major deviations from the status quo. For example, managers at BigCo are familiar with how to use a particular computer program and resist using an alternative, even though their program is outdated. Their resistance is driven more by their reluctance to learn something new than by the quality of the system itself.

- **Bias toward confirming our opinion.** Once we form an opinion, we typically seek out information that supports our viewpoint and ignore facts that may challenge it. For example, Dinah searches the Internet to find data supporting her preference for focus groups in market research, but she does not stop to read information that supports other approaches.

> **COGNITIVE BIAS** *n* 1: a systematic error introduced into sampling or testing by selecting or encouraging one outcome or answer over others

How do you prevent these biases from adversely affecting your decision-making ability? The best way is to recognize them, by ensuring that contrarian, diverse voices get introduced into the discussion.

"We tend to subconsciously decide what to do before figuring out why we want to do it."
—John S. Hammond, Ralph L. Keeney, and Howard Raiffa

Managing group dynamics

One of the advantages to treating decision making as a group process is that individual biases can be counteracted by the presence of multiple voices and perspectives.

But while groups offer different viewpoints, they need guidance to be productive. Your challenge is to *manage* the group decision-making process. Otherwise, you may find yourself confronted with one of the following extremes.

- **Excessive group harmony.** Excessive group harmony occurs when individuals want to be accepted in a group or they lack interest in the process. When people strive too hard to be accepted in the group, they may fall victim to *groupthink*. With groupthink, participants' desire for agreement overrides their motivation to evaluate alternative options. In this situation, people tend to withhold their opinions, especially if their views differ from those of the group leader. They make little effort to obtain new information from experts, and they selectively filter information to support their initial preferences. They may spend a lot of time inquiring about what others in the group want so that the solution they reach will make everyone happy.

Excessive group harmony can also stem from lack of interest: participants have no interest in the process or do not feel empowered. If the group feels that the leader has already made the decision, they may go along with it, refuse to participate entirely, or accept the first reasonable alternative that is proposed in an effort to end the process.

- **Excessive individualism.** Excessive individualism is at the opposite end of the spectrum from excessive group harmony. In this situation, individuals engage in aggressive advocacy, placing stakes in the ground and relentlessly arguing their positions. They disregard the opinions of other group members and fail to consider the common good.

Either of these extreme behaviors can lengthen the decision-making process and interfere with the team's effort to make good choices. Your job as a manager is to keep your decision-making group on track so it does not head toward either of these extremes.

Step 3: Framing the Issue at Hand

ONCE YOU'VE SET the stage and recognized common obstacles that can stand in the way of decision making, you're ready to frame the issue for your decision-making team. A key task during this step is to avoid the common error of seeking out solutions before you understand the nature (the root cause) of the issue at hand.

Distinguishing between symptoms and root causes

Consider the following story: New Age Electronics, a toy manufacturer, has a support phone line to answer customers' questions about assembling its products. The volume of phone calls has increased so much that the phone-support associates can't keep up with the demand. Customers have complained about waiting as long as half an hour to get help. Tai, the manager responsible for the support line, puts together a team to help him decide how to address the issue. He begins the first meeting by saying, "We have a serious problem with our customer support line. Customers are waiting too long for service. We need to fix it."

Because Tai has framed the issue as a problem with the phone-line response time, the team is most likely to focus on ways to reduce the response time—for example, adding more phone lines, adding more phone representatives, or increasing the hours of service. These solutions will address the *symptoms* of the problem—overloaded phone lines—but may not address the *root* of the problem.

Tip: When you're having a difficult time understanding the problem, consider moving to a new setting as this might trigger new insights.

To get to the root of the problem, Tai's team should be thinking about *why* customer calls have increased dramatically. Is one product in particular responsible for an inordinate number of calls? Is there a flaw in the design of a product or in the assembly instructions? Are the phone-support associates poorly trained? Suppose Tai had framed the issue by saying, "We have a serious problem with our customer support line. The volume of calls has increased, customers are waiting too long for service, and we need to find out why. Then we need to decide what to do about it." This framing would better guide the team toward uncovering the root cause of the problem. The team would thus stand a better chance of eventually deciding on a course of action that would address the cause of the problem instead of just treating a symptom of the problem.

Performing a root-cause analysis

To ensure that you get to the core of a problem, perform a root-cause analysis. During this process, you repeatedly make a statement of fact and ask the question *why*.

For example, Carla, the general manager of a pizza parlor, noticed that she was losing sales because her home deliveries were slower than her competitor's. Her friend suggests that they invest in a fleet of delivery vehicles to solve this problem. Instead of jumping to this conclusion, Carla asks, "Our pizza deliveries are slow. Why? Our delivery associates drive old cars that are in poor condition. Why? They can't afford repairs or newer cars. Why? They don't have the money. Why? Their pay is too low." Through this process, she realizes that the older, poorly maintained vehicles are a symptom of lower wages than those competitors paid.

Tip: When looking for the cause of a problem, look for something that changed at the same time the problem arose—you'll often find the cause there.

Root-cause analysis can work well for an individual, a small group, or in brainstorming sessions.

A tool that can help you perform such an analysis is called a *fishbone diagram*. As the figure, "Fishbone diagram" demonstrates, every fishbone diagram will look a little different, depending on the particular problem being solved.

When confronted with a problem, think about how to frame the issue for your team. Be careful not to assume from the outset that you know what the problem is. Challenge yourself and your team to get at the core of the issue by framing the problem in a variety of different ways and assessing whether the available

Fishbone diagram

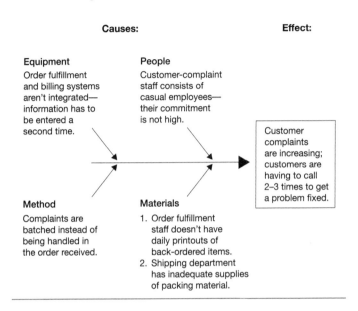

Causes: **Effect:**

Equipment
Order fulfillment
and billing systems
aren't integrated—
information has to
be entered a
second time.

People
Customer-complaint
staff consists of
casual employees—
their commitment
is not high.

Customer
complaints
are increasing;
customers are
having to call
2–3 times to get
a problem fixed.

Method
Complaints are
batched instead of
being handled in
the order received.

Materials
1. Order fulfillment
   staff doesn't have
   daily printouts of
   back-ordered items.
2. Shipping department
   has inadequate supplies
   of packing material.

information supports your theories. Throughout the entire process, ask *why* and other open-ended questions (those not requiring simply a yes or no response). Such questions encourage exploration more than closed questions based on predefined assumptions about the problem or requiring a yes or no response.

"If you have a 'yes man' working for you, one of you is redundant."
—Barry Rand, former CEO, Avis

Articulating your decision-making objectives

Once you have successfully framed the issue at hand, identify your objectives in determining a course of action. Ask your team questions like "What do you want the decision we make to accomplish?" and "What would you like to see happen as a result of the decision we reach?" Invite group members to describe their vision of the outcome of the decision as vividly and specifically as possible.

For example, if you were the manager at New Age Electronics, you and your team might come up with the following objectives:

- Reduce the average waiting time per customer to two minutes.

- Reduce call volume by 40 percent.

- Reduce average call duration to three minutes.

During the objective-setting process, you may encounter significant differences in opinion from one person to another. This is a healthy part of the dialogue and should be encouraged. However, if you find your list of objectives spiraling out of control, you may want to revisit the issue you're trying to address. You may find that you have more than one issue to resolve.

Once you have created a list of objectives, it's time to think about the possible courses of action you may take to achieve those goals.

Steps for Identifying Decision-Making Objectives

1. **Specify the objectives you want to reach.**

   What are you trying to achieve by making a decision? Make sure that as many people as possible with a stake in solving the problem are asked to specify their objectives. If you find you're hearing two or more substantially different objectives, you may conclude you're actually facing two or more problems, or that more than a few stakeholders don't understand the problem, or that different groups hope to see the problem solved in very different ways.

2. **Define—as specifically as possible—the performance level that represents a successful outcome.**

   Do you want a solution that boosts sales? By what percentage? For all regions? Be as precise as you can be.

3. **"Paint" a picture of what things will look like when the problem is solved.**

   Invite all stakeholders to describe the desired future state in as much detail as possible. Let imaginations and creativity run loose. Here, too, you may find significant divergence from one person to another. You may resolve differences by compromise, by straight selection of one view over another, or by determining that you in fact have two or more problems at hand.

4. **Make sure your agreed-on objectives and outcomes are not in conflict.**

   You may have determined that part of your solution to customer complaints about telephone orders is to have all of your phone-order reps take an additional three weeks of training. Another part of the solution is to reduce standards for each rep's completed orders per hour from eight to seven. But can you have the lower staffing levels due to training and the fewer customers handled by each rep at the same time? Will customers then complain more about long waits to have their orders taken? If yes, goals may have to be adjusted.

Step 4: Generating Alternatives

T O MAKE AN INFORMED decision, you need choices—alternative courses of action you might take to resolve the issue at hand. Generating alternatives creates those choices. After weighing the merits of a variety of options, you are in a better position to make the best decision for the situation facing you. Here, it's important to recognize that a "go/no-go" choice does not mean you have generated multiple alternatives—go/no-go is only a single option.

Consider the following story:

Paul, a marketing manager at a consumer products company, calls a meeting with his team to discuss how to increase laundry detergent sales in Latin America. The meeting begins with silence as everyone waits for someone else to speak. Paul breaks the silence by suggesting they consider changing the current packaging. Following this cue, someone chimes in with supporting statistics about packaging and consumer trends. Another person then describes the packaging of a product that has done well in Latin America. The meeting concludes with the assignment of a task force to research new packaging options.

This meeting seemed to proceed smoothly. But something's wrong. Paul didn't engage the team in generating alternatives. He didn't promote healthy debate or constructive conflict. Instead, excessive group harmony resulted in an action step based on the first idea that emerged: investigate packaging options. There was little creativity or innovative thinking. As a result, no *new* ideas surfaced. The group settled on the first alternative suggested, which had been Paul's idea!

Paul could have helped his group generate a wider range of promising alternatives if he had applied certain practices, such as brainstorming, dialoguing, and promoting fair process.

Brainstorming

Brainstorming is an effective way to generate different ideas and courses of action. How do you brainstorm? Start with a blank flip chart page. At the start of a meeting, ask your team members to suggest any ideas that come into their heads. Or ask individuals to take a few minutes to develop their own lists of ideas to share publicly.

Either way, record the ideas but don't discuss their merits at this point. Be especially careful not to allow criticism in the early stages. Instead, focus on identifying as many alternatives as possible. You can evaluate the ideas *after* you have a list of possibilities.

Tip: Before brainstorming, write the problem, issue, or question the group will brainstorm on a chalkboard or flip chart, where everyone can see it throughout the session. Get agreement from everyone that the issue is stated correctly and precisely.

Encouraging productive dialogue

Energize your team so that they will work hard to identify creative solutions. Creative conflict is essential to the generation of alternatives, but it should never be personal or divisive. Promote team participation during your brainstorming sessions by employing the following tactics:

- Encourage open, candid dialogue by making it clear at the outset that the final outcome is not predetermined and that everyone's input will be valued.

- Suggest that people try to think outside of their individual or departmental roles. They should focus on what's best for the group, using all of the available information.

- Provide closure at the end of every meeting by assigning tasks and deadlines so people are accountable for moving the process forward.

- Recognize and thank people who share their ideas and viewpoints in a positive manner—especially those who are willing to take the risk of challenging you.

Tip: Ask team members to play devil's advocate by researching and making a case against their preferred proposal. Ask them to explain in detail why the preferred option should *not* be adopted.

Promoting fair process

Throughout the decision-making process, it is essential that your team members feel that the process is fair. Specifically, they must believe that their ideas were acknowledged and considered, even if their suggestions were not ultimately adopted. This sense of fairness is critical for ensuring cooperation and buy-in when it comes time to implement the group's decision.

Alternatives provide the choices you will need to make an informed decision. When you encourage team participation, facilitate creative conflict, and listen to ideas, you are likely to generate a full slate of options that will serve you well as you enter the next step in the decision-making process: evaluating the alternatives your group has generated.

Tip: Either take notes yourself or appoint a note taker to show that you are considering everyone's ideas and that their input is valued and respected.

Step 5: Evaluating Alternatives

ONCE YOUR GROUP HAS generated alternatives to consider, it's time to evaluate those alternatives and select one as the final decision. How to pick the best solution? Your group can weigh a range of variables as well as use one or more systematic methods for reaching a decision: the prioritization matrix, the trade-off technique, or the decision tree.

Weighing a range of variables

To evaluate the alternatives your group has generated, members can take stock of how well each alternative meets the objectives you established at the outset of the decision-making process. The table "Variables for evaluating an alternative" shows examples.

Variables for evaluating an alternative

Variable	Questions to ask
Costs	• How much will this alternative cost? • Will it result in a cost savings now or over the long term? • Are there any hidden costs? • Are there likely to be additional costs down the road? • Does this alternative meet budget constraints?
Benefits	• What kind of profits will we realize if we implement this alternative? • Will it increase the quality of our product? • Will customer satisfaction increase?

Variable	Questions to ask
Intangibles	• Will our reputation improve if we implement this alternative? • Will our customers and/or our employees be more loyal?
Time	• How long will it take to implement this alternative? • Could there be delays? If so, what impact will this have on any schedules?
Feasibility	• Can this alternative be implemented realistically? • Are there any obstacles that must be overcome? • If this alternative is implemented, what resistance might be encountered inside or outside the organization?
Resources	• How many people are needed to implement this alternative? • Are they available? • What other projects will suffer if individuals focus on this option?
Risks	• What are the risks associated with this alternative? • Could this option result in loss of profits or competitive advantage? • Will competitors respond? If so, how?
Ethics	• Is this alternative legal? • Is it in the best interests of the customers, the employees, and the community where we operate? • Would I feel comfortable if other people knew about this alternative?

Using a prioritization matrix

Another method for evaluating alternatives is to create a prioritization matrix. To create the matrix:

1. List your objectives for making the decision at hand.

2. Assign each objective a value (highest = best).

3. Make each objective, along with its corresponding value, a column header for your matrix.

4. Make each alternative a row.

5. For each alternative, rate the objectives on a scale of 1 to 10 (10 = best).

6. Multiply your ratings by the priority values.

7. Add all the scores for each alternative to determine which has the highest number. This is your best decision, based on your priorities.

The table "Sample prioritization matrix" shows an example of how one group filled out a prioritization matrix.

Analyzing trade-offs

Like a prioritization matrix, a trade-off table can help you evaluate the various alternatives you've generated for the decision. The "Sample trade-off table" displays an example.

Sample prioritization matrix

	Increase profits (4)	Maintain low customer costs (3)	Implement quickly (2)	Use few internal resources (1)	Total score
Alternative A	9 x 4 = 36	2 x 3 = 6	7 x 2 = 14	2 x 1 = 2	**58**
Alternative B	2 x 4 = 8	9 x 3 = 27	8 x 2 = 16	3 x 1 = 3	**54**

What Would YOU Do?

Is That *Really* the Way the Cookie Crumbles?

L YLE IS A BRAND manager at a consumer products company, currently managing a gourmet cookie product. Sales of the cookie have been flat for the past eighteen months. Marketing studies have shown that only a limited number of consumers are willing to pay a premium price for a box of cookies, regardless of the quality. Lyle is faced with the challenge of increasing sales without diluting his brand's image. Senior management has made it clear that Lyle needs to find a solution fast.

Lyle assembles a group of five people to identify ways to increase revenues without diluting the cookie brand's image. The group has a mix of people with different backgrounds and levels of expertise. Three of the participants are from his staff, one is from sales, and the other is from research and development. The group explores options ranging from initiating a coupon program to reducing prices to forging corporate partnerships. After thorough discussion and analysis, the team decides that forming a partnership with another company is the most promising option.

Lyle identifies several ice cream companies as potential partners for creating a new (and hopefully best-selling) product: an ice cream sandwich with whimsical images of animals printed on the cookie portions of the confection. While he's in the early stages of researching these companies, Supreme Ice Cream approaches him about a partnership. Supreme is eager to move forward and is offering what appear to be very attractive terms for the deal. Lyle mulls over his next move. Should he grab the opportunity to partner with Supreme? Revisit the decision that a partnership is the best option for increasing revenues? Seek out other offers and then evaluate the Supreme deal? The whole thing has begun to feel as opaque as a bowl of cookie batter.

What would YOU do? See *What You COULD Do*.

Sample trade-off table

	Profits	Customer costs	Time to implement	Internal resources
Alternative A	Profits increase by $100,000	Cost to customer increases by $1 per unit	6 months to implement	20 people required
Alternative B	Profits increase by $10,000	Cost to customer increases by $0	4 months to implement	15 people required

Once you lay out the alternatives with their associated information, consider how important these factors are to your group and/or the company, and identify the compromises that you are willing to make.

For example, would a $90,000 increase in profits be worth the time of five extra people?

Be sure to think about the trade-offs in light of the priority you assign to each objective.

Using a decision tree

Decision trees are another form of systematic approach to evaluating alternatives. Consider a situation in which you project an increased demand for your product. You and your team need to decide whether to continue manufacturing a component internally or whether to outsource the work. The figure, "Decision tree," shown on the next page presents a simplified view of your alternatives.

According to this simplified decision tree, the best course of action would be to pursue alternative B. (Of the two options, alternative B offers the highest risk-adjusted net present value.)

"When you come to a fork in the road, take it."
—Yogi Berra

Decision trees are typically much more robust than the one in the previous figure in that they evaluate more options and include

Decision tree

Alternative A

Keep the work in-house. Cost per unit remains the same, but the number of products developed is limited. No jobs are eliminated.

Demand increases. Research suggests probability is 80%.

Your company can't keep up with orders and may lose business to competitors. Prices remain the same. The net present value of expected change to profits, including investment costs, is –$1M.

Demand decreases. Research suggests probability is 20%.

Your company is able to fulfill orders and keep costs low. The net present value of expected change to profits, including investment costs, is –$0.

Alternative B

Outsource the work. Cost per unit increases, but more products can be developed. Manufacturing jobs are eliminated.

Demand increases. Research suggests probability is 50%.

You are able to meet the demand and sell more products. You may or may not have to raise prices to cover your additional costs. The net present value of expected change to profits, including investment costs, is $500K.

Demand decreases. Research suggests probability is 50%.

You have to raise prices to cover additional costs to make less from each sale. Sales stay flat. The net present value of expected change to profits, including investment costs, is –$500K.

◇ Decision point

○ Uncertain event

multiple decision points. In general, the more alternatives you consider, and the more detailed a decision tree you can create, the more likely you are to discover a solution that meets your needs. However, a decision tree won't automatically indicate the best course of action—you'll still need to assess the information in the decision tree to make the wisest choice.

Tip: Encourage constructive contention by inviting others to challenge your opinions and ideas: "My perspective on this is _____; however, I may be wrong. Could you identify any gaps in my logic so we can come up with the most effective decision?"

What You COULD Do.

Remember Lyle's uncertainty about how to respond to Supreme Ice Cream's offer of a partnership deal?

While it might be tempting to move ahead and establish a partnership immediately with Supreme, it is too early for Lyle to do so at this time. Lyle should wait until other offers have been submitted and evaluate the Supreme Ice Cream offer in relation to those offers. Also, Lyle shouldn't reconvene his group to revisit the decision that a partnership is the best option for increasing revenues. The group has already made its decision. If Lyle reopens the discussion, he runs the risk of taking too much time and missing an opportunity to partner with Supreme Ice Cream. Rehashing old decisions often results in stalled efforts to move forward.

Lyle and his group should pursue other offers and compare them with Supreme Ice Cream's proposal. Evaluating multiple offers will give them a better context in which to make a choice. After careful review, Lyle and his group might realize that Supreme Ice Cream's offer was not as attractive as they originally thought.

Step 6: Making the Decision

I N A PERFECT WORLD, you would have all of the information you need and an unlimited amount of time to make a decision. Your choices would be clear, and company politics would not influence your decision. Often, however, you need to make complex decisions quickly, with only partial information. The techniques for evaluating the alternatives outlined in the previous section should help you compare the pros and cons of each choice. But what if your group is still having difficulty arriving at a final decision—and the clock is ticking? The following suggestions can help.

Moving toward closure

If your group is having difficulty reaching a final decision, consider using the following methods to help the team move toward resolution:

- **Point-counterpoint.** Divide your team into two groups of equal size: group A and group B. Wherever possible, spread supporters of opposing ideas between the groups. Ask group A to develop a proposal for a solution that includes their recommendations and key assumptions. Then have them present their proposal to group B. Then ask group B to identify one or more alternative plans of action and present those plans to group A. Have both groups debate the different proposals until they all agree on a set of recommendations.

For example, a finance department has been engaged in a heated debate over which accounting firm to use to audit the books this year. One group favors a big-name brand, while the other favors a smaller yet well-respected firm. Using the point-counterpoint technique, the decision-making team considers each firm and reaches a conclusion.

- **Intellectual watchdog.** Divide your team into two groups of equal size. Group A develops a proposal for a solution that includes their recommendations and key assumptions. They then present their proposal to group B. Instead of having group B generate an alternative plan of action, ask group B to critique the proposal and present its analysis to group A. Ask group A to revise the proposal on the basis of group B's feedback and present it again. The two groups continue to critique and revise the proposal until they agree on a set of recommendations.

For example, a manufacturer of office furniture needs to improve the quality of its products. The first group assumes that the problem with quality is due to outdated manufacturing equipment, and recommends investment in better equipment. The second group questions this assumption, critiques the proposal, and presents its analysis to the first group. The first group revises its proposal. The two groups work together in the revision-critique-revision cycle until they arrive at a solution that both groups think will improve their products' quality.

Here are some additional suggestions for resolving disagreements and moving your group toward closure:

- Revisit and retest the assumptions about the issue at hand.

- Go back to the original decision-making objectives and ensure that they are still appropriate.

- Set a deadline for coming to closure—for example, "By next Tuesday, we will make our decision, no matter how much uncertainty remains."

- Agree that if disagreements remain unresolved, the final choice will be made by a particular rule, such as majority voting, group consensus, or a decision by the senior-most member of the group.

Ending the deliberations

Knowing when to end deliberations can be difficult. If a group makes a decision too early, it might not explore enough possibilities. If you sense that your group is rushing to make a decision, consider adjourning a meeting before making a final choice, and reconvening at a later time. Ask each participant to try to find a flaw with the decision to present at the next meeting.

The flip side of deciding too early is deciding too late, which is equally problematic. If the group takes too long to make a decision, it may waste valuable time and possibly even miss the opportunity to solve the problem at hand. If your team insists on hearing every viewpoint and resolving every question before reaching a conclusion, the result is the same: your discussions will become a tiring, endless loop. If you find your group is stuck going around in circles, it is your job as a manager to bring the discussion to closure. You may need to simply "force the issue" by establishing a deadline for a decision, urging your group to use the best information available within that time frame.

Step 7: Communicating the Decision

MANY MANAGERS OVERLOOK one of the most important steps in the decision-making process: communicating the decision to everyone who was involved in it and who will be affected by it. To communicate a decision effectively, you need to take the right approach and make sure you include all the right information in your messages about the decision.

Taking the right approach

Once your group has made a final choice, some members will have to give up their preferred solution. The fairness of the decision-making process as perceived by the participants and others will determine their willingness to support the final outcome. In communicating the decision and getting buy-in for its implementation, keep in mind the following principles:

- **Consideration and voice.** Participants who are encouraged to question and debate each other's ideas are more likely to believe that the leader listened to their viewpoints and gave them serious consideration. This is especially true if you, the leader, have demonstrated attentiveness through your actions—for example, by taking notes and playing back or paraphrasing what was said to show that you were actively listening. Even if some participants' viewpoints did not prevail, knowing that you took them seriously will lend credibility to the process and help everyone to accept the final decision.

- **Explanation.** You need to explain the thinking behind the final decision. It's important to be clear about why you and your group made *this* choice, as opposed to a different one. Explaining the reasons for the decision builds trust in your intentions and confidence that the final choice was made for the benefit of the company as a whole.

- **Expectation.** Once the decision has been made, everyone affected by the decision needs to understand the new rules of the game. Spell out new responsibilities as well as performance measures and penalties for failure to follow the decision. When people clearly understand what's expected of them after a decision has been made, they can focus on what they need to do to support the decision.

The people you notify will include everyone who is responsible for implementing the decision as well as anyone who will be affected by it. Your list might also include other key stakeholders: members of your unit who were not part of the decision-making group, senior management, department supervisors, external constituents, and even customers if they will see a change in the way your company does business with them as a result of the decision.

Including the right content in your message

Your messages about the decision should include the following components:

- Statement of the issue that needed to be addressed

- Description of the objectives or decision-making criteria

- The names and roles of the people involved in making the decision and why they were included in the process

- The alternatives considered (and possibly a summary of the evaluation in table form)

- An explanation of the final decision and what it means for the key stakeholders

- The implementation plan and time frame

- Recognition of those who participated

- Solicitation of feedback

Be sure to take the time to create a clear, concise message. Incomplete or poorly articulated messages about your group's decision can lead to confusion, disappointment, and unwillingness to support its implementation on the part of everyone who hears or reads your messages.

Step 8: Implementing the Decision

Y OUR GROUP HAS MADE a choice, and you've communicated the decision to the appropriate people. Now it's time to identify the tasks that will be required to put the decision into action, assign resources, and establish deadlines. Ideally, your team members will leave the final meeting knowing exactly what they're expected to do. If not, reconvene the group to identify who will be responsible for each task.

Assigning tasks, allocating resources

You probably have much of the information you need to develop the plan for implementing your group's decision. When you were evaluating alternatives, you likely considered the cost, the number of people required to work on the project, and so forth.

For example, suppose you and your group have determined that customer complaints about your telephone support line are due to inadequate training of the support associates taking calls. After analyzing the situation, you may decide that the associates need to have more product knowledge. As part of evaluating this alternative, you probably would have identified the resource requirements from the training department to implement your solution.

But be sure to assign reasonable tasks with sufficient resources. For example, the people in the training department may not have extensive product knowledge and may need the help of a content expert. You might need to assign an expert in product knowledge to work with the training department to develop a program.

Monitoring and following up

As you implement your decision, keep track of how things are going. The following practices can help:

- **Clarify expectations and acknowledge incentives.** For example, if an account executive is going to start managing the company's largest client, explain what this client means to the organization and your expectations for managing the relationship. Determine whether the increase in responsibility should result in a pay increase or change in title, and follow up with your human resource department to make that happen.

- **Provide feedback on the implementation.** Give your employees feedback on the progress of the implementation plan. Your input should be constructive and focused on accountability and execution. Set a time for daily or weekly status meetings. This will help you stay informed of your group's progress during implementation.

- **Take a look for yourself.** Check in with people informally. Ask them how the project is going and whether they have any concerns about it. Be interested in not only issues related to implementation, such as schedule and budget, but also whether your employees believe that the project is effectively addressing the problem it is intended to solve.

- **Recognize people's contributions.** Implementation often goes unnoticed unless it fails. If things are going well, recognize individual contributions and celebrate successes.

Keeping abreast of progress during implementation will enable you to fix problems before they become major crises.

Making needed adjustments

Most implementation plans require some adjustment. If nothing else, conditions change over time. So occasional adjustments, ranging from fine-tuning to wholesale changes, are often needed.

What if the decision you've implemented ultimately doesn't work out as you'd expected? In most cases, corrections can be made. These will often involve only "tweaking" the decision you've implemented. But sometimes you may find that the alternative you chose just isn't working. In such cases, you need to revisit the decision-making process.

- Make sure you framed the issue correctly. Have you learned anything new that makes you think the problem is different from what you thought the first time around?

- Has there been a change in your objectives? Do you have new information that you didn't have before? Perhaps you see that one objective should have been given more weight and another one less.

- Have you learned about an alternative that wasn't considered the first time around? Or have you acquired a different perspective that causes you to reassess data you've had for some time?

- Go through your decision-making process again, preferably without reviewing your earlier results. With experience in implementing one alternative, chances are good you'll change your opinion of how well some of the other alternatives satisfy your objectives.

After you've evaluated how well each alternative would be expected to address each objective, return to the results of your first evaluation. Where you find discrepancies between the first time and this time, decide which one is more on target in light of what you know now.

Assessing Your Decision-Making Process

MANY MANAGERS WAIT TO evaluate a decision until the end of the process, after it has been implemented. This is too late. If there is a flaw in the decision itself or in its implementation, you may learn a useful lesson about how *not* to make or implement a decision, but it will be too late to repair the damage.

Assessing the decision-making process is an ongoing effort that must occur in real time, throughout all the phases of the process. For example, you need to monitor the tone of your meetings and address problems in group dynamics *before* they interfere with your goal. Sometimes new information becomes available or new conditions arise, necessitating a midcourse correction in your objectives.

Have a plan for evaluating the various elements in your process, from gathering your decision-making team to implementing the actual decision. It could be something as simple as a checklist. Take the time after each meeting to think about how it went. In addition, understand the distinguishing characteristics of effective decision making.

Understanding the five characteristics of effective decision making

Research suggests decisions that include these five process characteristics have sharply improved the odds of being successful:

- **Multiple alternatives.** Generally, successful decisions result from a review of many alternative solutions. As your process unfolds, make sure that your group considers several alternatives before making its decision. The point-counterpoint approach is a useful method to ensure that at least two alternatives are considered. Remember, a go/no-go choice involves only one alternative.

- **Open debate.** To generate creative alternatives, you need to facilitate open, constructive debate. Strive to create an environment that supports inquiry-based discussions. Ask open-ended and hypothetical questions to encourage your group to explore a variety of possibilities. Listen attentively to your team's suggestions, and emphasize positive group dynamics. Debate should be task related, not emotional or personal. Make adjustments to your approach if the group is not working well together. Silence and suppressed arguments are both signs that the debate is not sufficiently robust.

- **Assumption testing.** It is unlikely that you will have complete information at the time you make your decision. Your group will have to make assumptions as it proceeds. Make sure that your team recognizes when it is relying on facts and when it is making assumptions. Further, the team needs to recognize which of those assumptions are closely tied to confirmed data, and which are not. The group may still choose to use untested assumptions in its decision-making process, but should reconsider the plausibility of these assumptions throughout the process.

- **Well-defined objectives.** Continually review your objectives during your meetings to ensure that your discussions stay on target. If conditions change, you may need to refine your objectives or even your definition of the problem to meet the new conditions. However, don't let your objectives shift solely because of time pressure or a rush to reach agreement.

- **Perceived fairness.** Keeping people involved throughout the process is critical to the success of your decision. Your team members must feel that their ideas are being considered *during* the process in order to feel a sense of ownership over the final decision. Periodically evaluate the level of participation of your team members, such as after a milestone. If people have stopped participating in conversations or are doing so reluctantly, they may be dissatisfied with the process. Your job is to keep people engaged by acknowledging your team members' suggestions and helping them understand why another alternative may be a better decision.

Paying careful attention to these characteristics throughout the decision-making process can be difficult and time-consuming. Making the effort to include them, however, gives your decision a much better chance of success.

In addition to demonstrating five distinguishing process characteristics, effective decisions are ethical. Let's examine this more closely in the following section.

Making ethical decisions

Whenever you make a decision, particularly a complex one, it will almost certainly affect other people. The consequences will be social as well as economic. Ethics and company values will often be at stake. For example, Radu, a manager of a customer-service phone line at a company that manufactures a new medical monitoring device, has been told that he needs to cut costs. The company is in financial trouble and has to cut costs across the board to stay afloat. Radu's team decides that the alternative that will result in the most savings is to charge customers for phone calls and to reduce the number of hours the line is open. Before making the final decision, however, the group should consider whether that option is a good balance between the interests of the company and those of the customer who may need help using the monitor.

Very few complex decisions can be made on the basis of cost alone. Most decisions involve considering a variety of factors. And these decisions require sound judgment on your part in weighing those factors. As a manager, you need to assess the consequences of your alternatives as best you can and then make a decision.

Ethics should play an important part in your team's deliberations *before* the group makes a decision. Ask your group to explicitly consider ethical issues according to their own values—and not dismiss them as "soft" and therefore unworthy of discussion. For instance, if a team member feels uncomfortable because she heard rumors that the highly successful company you are considering working with overseas has been polluting the environment, she should be encouraged to bring her concerns to the table for deliberation.

One technique to ensure that ethics are considered during your discussions is to appoint an "ethical watchdog," or ombudsman. The person who fills this role would be responsible for ensuring that ethical issues surface during discussions. During the course of the decision-making process, the role of ethical watchdog should rotate periodically.

There is no set of universal guidelines for making ethical decisions. However, a starting point might include asking questions such as "Which option will produce the greatest good and do the least harm?"

At a minimum, make sure that your decision passes the following two tests:

- **The legal test.** The decision is not against the law or against company regulations. For example, it does not discriminate against anyone on the basis of race, gender, age, or religion. You may also want to consider whether something that is technically legal goes against your company's regulations. To illustrate, your company may have a policy that its facilities must comply with all U.S. environmental regulations, even if the facility is located in a country or region where the environmental standards are more relaxed than in the United States.

- **The stakeholder test.** The decision is in the best interest of the company's employees, customers, community, and other key stakeholders, such as federal or state regulators. Sometimes a decision that doesn't directly increase profits is actually in the company's best interest. For instance, a pharmaceutical company's decision to provide low-cost prescriptions to elderly and low-income customers may cost money up front, but it significantly improves the company's brand image, which eventually leads to increased profits in the future.

If your decision passes the two tests above, as a final check, you might want to consider what someone you respect would say if you told them you chose a particular option.

Another key to evaluating the ethics of an option is to consider whether the decision-making and implementation process is open and direct. If you find yourself uncomfortable with the idea that other people will know about the decision, you may *not* be making the ethical choice.

Some companies develop statements about their values and ethical principles. These statements may include goals such as providing top-quality products, reducing waste to the environment, and fostering an open, honest, and direct corporate culture. While you can refer to the company's value statement for guidance, it is unlikely that this document will be enough. You will probably have to use your personal judgment as well.

For example, suppose you have to decide what to do about an employee who has a drug problem. In this case, you may decide that the cost of getting help for this person (e.g., lost time on the job) is outweighed by the value of this person's skills or expertise to your group and your company.

In sum, important decisions cannot be based on financial considerations alone. As a manager, you need to consider the wider ethical dimensions of the decision. That means weighing the consequences of a decision in the broader context of the law, as well as the individuals and community it will affect.

Tools
and
Resources

Tools and Resources
for Leading People

Self-Evaluation: Characteristics of Effective Leadership

The questions below relate to characteristics of effective leaders. Use the questions to evaluate whether you possess these characteristics. Use the results to see where you might focus to strengthen your leadership skills.

Characteristics of Effective Leaders	Yes	No
Future-focused		
1. Do you have a clear vision?		
2. Have you made your vision clear to your group?		
Persistent; tenacious		
3. When pursuing a goal, do you maintain a positive, focused attitude, despite obstacles?		
Comfortable with ambiguity		
4. Are you willing to take calculated risks?		
5. Are you comfortable with a certain level of disruption and conflict?		
Excellent communicators		
6. Do you listen closely (rather than have a response ready before the other person finishes)?		
7. Are you comfortable running meetings?		
8. Are you comfortable making presentations and speaking in public?		
9. Do you have the skills needed to negotiate in a variety of settings?		
Politically astute		
10. Could you diagram for yourself your organization's actual power structure?		
11. Can you articulate the concerns of your organization's most powerful groups?		
12. Can you identify those individuals within your organization who will support you when needed?		
13. Do you know where to turn for the resources you need?		

Characteristics of Effective Leaders	Yes	No
Self-aware		
14. Are you aware of or can you describe how your own patterns of behavior affect others?		
Level-headed		
15. In situations that are full of turmoil and confusion, do you stay calm and level-headed?		
Caring		
16. Do you empathize with other people's needs, concerns, and professional goals?		
17. Would staff members confirm that you show such empathy?		
Able to use humor		
18. Do you know how to use humor to relieve tense or uncomfortable situations?		

If you answered "yes" to most of these questions, you have the characteristics of an effective leader.

If you answered "no" to some or many of these questions, you may want to consider how you can further develop these effective leadership characteristics.

Worksheet for Crafting and Maintaining Your Vision

Complete this worksheet to create a "picture" of your hoped-for vision: what it will look like, how it will function, what it will produce. Use the results to maintain a record of your vision and help sell it to others.

1. Gather Information for the Vision

Write a general description of the hoped-for end result.

What information is necessary to define the vision in detail?

Who across the organization can provide information, input, and early support? What do you need to ask them?

Input and ideas:

Who might oppose this effort? What questions do you need to ask them?

Feedback:

2. Craft the Vision

Articulate the vision.

What is your overall strategy to reach the vision?

3. Checklist: Is Your Vision Realistic?	Yes	No
1. Have team members contributed to the vision and given "buy-in"?		
2. Is the vision realistic and achievable?		
3. Does the end-result of the vision serve the interests of the company's most important stakeholders?		
4. Does the vision include a clear definition of the benefits to all the constituencies that might be affected?		
5. Is the language used in the vision documentation easy to explain and understand?		
6. Does the description of the vision include and articulate a wide range of perspectives (of all affected stakeholders)?		
If you answer "no" to any question, revisit the vision and adjust it to include that aspect.		

Establishing Credibility

Use this checklist to evaluate how well you are able to establish credibility and to create a prodcutive working environment.

Checklist for Establishing Credibility	Yes	No
1. Do you have, and can you demonstrate competence in a particular area?		
2. Do you demonstrate your willingness to work hard on a day-to-day basis?		
3. Do you use whatever power and influence you have to benefit others?		
4. Do you consciously treat everyone with whom you come in contact consistently and fairly?		
5. Do you focus on practicing active listening on a day-to-day basis?		
6. Do you keep track of and deliver on all promises you make?		
7. Do you consistently meet deadlines?		
8. Do you remain calm under pressure?		
9. Do you prepare thoroughly for meetings and presentations?		
10. Do you answer all phone calls and respond to all e-mails promptly?		
11. Do you keep accurate and detailed records of projects and activities?		
12. Would colleagues at any level say they have never heard you put another person down?		
13. Do you show that you will not tolerate "scapegoating," or misapplied blame?		
14. Do you listen fairly, kindly and with courtesy to the opinions of others?		
15. Do you respect other people's ideas and give each one the same amount of consideration, regardless of level?		

Checklist for Establishing Credibility	Yes	No
16. Do you go to bat for your team to get the resources you need?		
17. Do you shelter your team from interference and show courage in sticking up for your people?		
18. Do you protect voices of dissent, and leaders who are working without authority?		
19. Do you admit it when you make a mistake or when you don't have the answer?		
20. Do you use every reasonable opportunity to foster other's professional growth?		

*If you answer **"yes"** to most of these questions, you are probably doing a good job of establishing your credibility and building a productive work environment.*

*If you answer **"no"** to any questions, you may want to focus on how to improve your performance in that area. Identify how to change your behavior and practice it until it becomes second nature.*

Keeping Staff and Allies Motivated

Complete this worksheet regularly to track how motivated staff and allies are and to consider how well you are using available strategies to keep them motivated.

Date:

Staff morale is   *(Up? Down? Flat? Mixed?)* **because**

Successes or major milestones we have achieved so far:

Individuals who have been instrumental in success to date and what motivates them:

Reward ideas for group:

Aspects of the "big picture" to emphasize at this point in the effort:

Checklist: How Well Are You Maintaining Motivation?	Yes	No
1. Have you offered feedback and recognition to individuals who have been instrumental in successes to date?		
2. Have you reported to the team and allies about successes achieved so far and how they relate to the big picture?		
3. Have you celebrated successes and the accomplishment of major milestones?		
4. Have you spoken recently about the team's ability to overcome problems?		
5. Have you spoken to team members about the importance of their work and how it relates to the company's or unit's larger goals?		
6. Have you remembered to offer special rewards, such as food at team meetings or achievement awards?		
*If you answer "**no**" to any question, consider adjusting your leadership strategies.*		

Test Yourself

Test Yourself offers ten multiple-choice questions to help you identify your baseline knowledge of leading and motivating.

Answers to the questions are given at the end of the test.

1. As a leader, you should rely on others for help.

  a. True.

  b. False.

2. A leader's primary job is to

  a. Create a clear and enduring set of strategic objectives.

  b. Influence others.

  c. Meet the challenges of the future.

3. A charismatic leader is most successful during times when

  a. There is a downturn in the economy.

  b. The company is negotiating a merger.

  c. A labor strike threatens production.

4. To learn how to become a leader, you can

   a. Ask to take on challenging projects.

   b. Prepare by being the best manager you can.

   c. Find a mentor in a different field.

5. What is NOT a characteristic of an effective leader?

   a. Excellent communication skills.

   b. A sense of humor.

   c. Dislike of ambiguity.

6. You are focusing on developing your leadership skills. Is being politically astute about your organization's power structure and using what you know a characteristic of being an effective leader?

   a. Yes.

   b. No.

   c. Sometimes, but you don't want to rely on outsiders for support.

7. A democratic leadership style is characterized by

   a. Coaching talented direct reports.

   b. Achieving consensus in a group.

   c. Maintaining a "people first" approach to leading.

8. An effective leader's vision needs to be

   a. Daring and exciting.

   b. A goal that can never quite be reached.

   c. Simple and enduring.

9. To motivate people, a leader should

   a. Celebrate successes.

   b. Never allow any questioning of the vision.

   c. Be willing to adjust the vision as needed.

10. An effective leader

   a. Will never show emotions.

   b. Does not admit mistakes.

   c. Finds a sanctuary to let go and relax.

Answers to test questions

1, a. Yes, of course, you should rely on others. You can't do it all yourself. The people within your own group—whether that group is a company, department, or team—are critical for achieving your vision.

2, b. Leaders need to persuade, influence, and motivate others. A leader also creates a vision for change—strategic objectives follow the vision.

3, c. Charismatic leaders function best during a time of crisis, not during ongoing situations.

4, a. Find challenging projects to learn new ways of seeing problems and solutions. Don't just stay at the managerial level, and don't connect with an inappropriate mentor.

5, c. Leaders have to be comfortable with the unknown; ambiguity is an inherent element of the future, and leaders have to be future-focused.

6, a. Do be politically astute. Effective leaders know their organization's power structure. They listen carefully to concerns of centers of power, and they know where to go for resources and support they need.

7, b. A democratic leadership is characterized by a leader working to achieve consensus in a group, often a difficult task.

8, c. An effective leader will have a vision that others can understand and accept as bringing about a better future.

9, a. Celebrate successes, large and small, at the start, the middle and the end of the road.

10, c. Leaders need to take care of themselves. Often they work too hard and take on too much stress. Finding a quiet place to relax and unwind is important for a leader's mental health.

To Learn More

Notes and Articles

Loren Gary. "Power: How Its Meaning in Corporate Life Is Changing." *Harvard Management Update*, October 1996.

This article offers a review of current literature on power and the way power is used by both individuals and organizations. The author shows the psychological transition in equating power as "not the capacity to destroy, but rather, the ability to influence others." He discusses the ways in which power is applied in various management situations and how you can use power to transform your relationships with others in an organization.

Daniel Goleman. "Leadership That Gets Results." *Harvard Business Review* OnPoint Enhanced Edition. Boston: Harvard Business School Publishing, 2000.

Drawing on research on more than 3,000 executives, Goleman explores which precise leadership behaviors yield positive results. He outlines six distinct leadership styles, each one arising from different components of emotional intelligence. For example, coercive leaders demand immediate compliance. Authoritative leaders mobilize people toward a vision. Affiliative leaders create emotional bonds and harmony. Democratic leaders build consensus through participation. Pacesetting leaders expect excellence and self-direction. And coaching leaders develop people for the future. The research indicates that leaders who get the best results don't rely on just one leadership style; they use most of the styles in any given week. Goleman maintains that with practice leaders can switch among leadership styles to produce powerful results, thus turning the art of leadership into a skill that can be learned.

Daniel Goleman, Richard Boyatzis, and Annie Mckee. "Primal Leadership: The Hidden Driver of Great Performance." *Harvard Business Review* OnPoint Enhanced Edition. Boston: Harvard Business School Publishing, 2001.

You've heard about the importance of emotional intelligence in the workplace—that there's an incontrovertible link between executives' emotional maturity, exemplified by such capabilities as self-awareness and empathy, and their financial performance. Now, new research extends that base. Drawing on two years of research, the authors contend that the leader's mood and his or her attendant behaviors have enormous effects on bottom-line performance. Accordingly, top executives' primary task is emotional leadership. Therefore, leaders must first attend to the impact of their moods and behaviors. To help them do that, the authors introduce a five-step process of self-reflection and planning.

Daniel Goleman. "What Makes a Leader?" *Harvard Business Review* OnPoint Enhanced Edition. Boston: Harvard Business School Publishing, 2000.

Superb leaders have very different ways of directing a team, a division, or a company. Some are subdued and analytical; others are charismatic and go with their gut. And different situations call for different types of leadership. Most mergers need a sensitive negotiator at the helm, whereas many turnarounds require a more forceful kind of authority. The author has found, however, that effective leaders are alike in one crucial way: They all have a high degree of what has come to be known as emotional intelligence. The components of emotional intelligence—self-awareness, self-regulation, motivation, empathy, and social skill—can sound unbusinesslike. But exhibiting emotional intelligence in the workplace does not mean simply controlling your anger or getting along with people. Rather, it means understanding your own and other people's emotional makeup well enough to move people in the direction of accomplishing your company's goals.

Harvard Business School Publishing. "How to Lead When You're Not the Boss." *Harvard Management Update*, March 2000.

If you're like most managers, you regularly find yourself in situations where you have the responsibility but not the authority to get things done through a group. Negotiation experts Roger Fisher and Alan Sharp have developed a leadership model called "lateral leadership," which allows a person to lead a group regardless of his or her formal role. Their five-step method includes setting clear objectives, thinking systematically, learning from experience, and being able to engage the other participants and give them effective feedback.

Harvard Business School Publishing. "Trust: How to Build It, Earn It—and Reestablish It When It's Broken." *Harvard Management Update*, September 2000.

In earlier decades, it may have been enough simply to understand the link between trust and financial performance on a theoretical level. Today, however, the demands are greater: The connection must be made actionable, and managers must be able to deploy trust in ways that yield tangible results. But before you can be trusted, you have to be willing to trust others. Try too earnestly to foster it, and your efforts can backfire, instilling suspicion among employees. What follows is some concrete advice for dealing with trust, an admittedly squishy subject. Includes the sidebar "How to Heal from Betrayal" and a list of additional resources.

Ronald A. Heifetz and Loren Gary. "The Work of a Modern Leader: An Interview with Ron Heifetz." *Harvard Management Update*, April 1997.

This interview explores organizational and individual resistance to the work of adaptive leadership, examining Heifetz's principles of "getting on the balcony" and "regulating distress" in some detail.

Linda Hill and Loren Gary. "What You Must Learn to Become a Manager: An Interview with Linda Hill." *Harvard Management Update*, July 1997.

Professor Hill explains the psychological transition that newly minted managers undergo. Beyond the change in functions, new managers are forced to adopt a new identity and to alter how they measure success.

John P. Kotter. "What Leaders Really Do." *Harvard Business Review* OnPoint Enhanced Edition. Boston: Harvard Business School Publishing, 2000.

Leadership and management are two distinctive and complementary systems of action, each with its own function and characteristic activities. Management involves coping with complexity, while leadership involves coping with change. Most U.S. corporations actively seek out people with leadership potential and expose them to career experiences designed to develop that potential.

Jennifer McFarland. "Leading Quietly." *Harvard Management Update*, July 2001.

Leaders are not always rough-and-ready heroes; rather, those who practice "tempered radical[ism]" can stay both inside and outside the system, pushing the organization to see new ways of thinking and learning. Leaders need to listen to those around them, especially those who have new ideas, radical or not.

Noel Tichy and Tom Brown. "Companies Don't Develop Leaders, CEOs Do: An Interview with Noel Tichy." *Harvard Management Update*, October 1997.

Professor Tichy discusses the importance of the CEO's role in leadership development. He asserts that the best people in the company to educate and develop future leaders are those who have a record of success that others can learn from.

Linda Klebe Trevino, Laura Pincus Hartman, and Michael Brown. "Moral Person and Moral Manager: How Executives Develop a Reputation for Ethical Leadership." *California Management Review*, July 2000.

Based on interviews with senior executives and corporate ethics officers, this article reveals that a reputation for executive ethical leadership rests on two essential pillars: the executive's visibility as a moral person (based on perceived traits, behaviors, and decision-making processes) and visibility as a moral manager (based on role modeling, use of the reward system, and communication). The article also offers guidelines for cultivating a reputation for ethical leadership.

Margaret Wheatley and Walter Kiechel. "The Dance of Change in Corporate America: An Interview with Margaret Wheatley." *Harvard Management Update*, November 1996.

Wheatley discusses the struggle occurring within American corporations between traditional structures and self-organizing forms, in which networks, patterns, and structures emerge without external imposition or direction. The role of a leader in an organization is changing profoundly. While some leaders have become more thoughtful, others feel threatened by the changes. Wheatley argues that the preservation of personal power and status is antithetical to learning organizations.

Abraham Zaleznik. "Managers and Leaders: Are They Different?" *Harvard Business Review* OnPoint Enhanced Edition. Boston: Harvard Business School Publishing, 2001.

Managers tend to exercise their skills in diplomacy and focus on decision-making processes within an organization. They wish to create an ordered corporate structure and are emotionally detached from their work. Leaders, in contrast, direct their energies toward introducing new approaches and ideas. Leaders engender excitement through their work and often realize their potential through one-to-one relationships with mentors. Business organizations can foster the development of leaders by establishing such relationships between junior and senior executives. This article includes a retrospective commentary by the author.

Books

Marvin Bower. *Will to Lead: Running a Business with a Network of Leaders.* Boston: Harvard Business School Press, 1997.

Although the command-and-control style of leadership once contributed to the building of America's might, Bower argues it is no longer the best system for today's intensely competitive global marketplace. People down the line don't like the system and don't do their best work under it. Moreover, command-and-control management breeds rigidity and excessive reliance on authority. Bower urges companies to shift away from managing through authority and hierarchy to running a business with a network of leaders and leadership teams dispersed strategically throughout the business. He describes the factors in designing a leadership company and explains how leadership can be learned on the job.

Daniel Goleman, Richard Boyatzis, and Annie McKee. *Primal Leadership: Realizing the Power of Emotional Intelligence.* Boston: Harvard Business School Press, 2002.

Daniel Goleman's international best-seller *Emotional Intelligence* forever changed our concept of "being smart," proving that emotional intelligence (EI)—how we handle ourselves and our relationships—matters more than IQ. His next book, *Working with Emotional Intelligence,* proved that personal career success also depends primarily on EI. Now, Goleman teams with Richard Boyatzis and Annie McKee—experts on the cutting edge of EI research—to explore the consequences of emotional intelligence for leaders and organizations. Unveiling scientific evidence that links organizational success or failure to "primal leadership," the authors argue that a leader's emotions are contagious and must resonate enthusiasm if an organization is to thrive.

Kurt Hanks. *Motivating People: How to Motivate Others to Do What You Want* and *Thank You for the Opportunity*. Menlo Park, CA: Crisp Publications, 1991.

This easy-to-read book contains succinct and practical tips on what motivates people and plenty of do's and don'ts in a well-organized format.

Harvard Business School Publishing. *Choosing the Right Leadership Style: No Single Approach Fits All Situations. Harvard Business Review* OnPoint Collection. Boston: Harvard Business School Publishing, 2001.

This collection of OnPoint-enhanced articles from *Harvard Business Review* explores the connections between leadership and performance improvement without settling on a "one-size-fits-all" prescription.

Harvard Business School Publishing. *Harvard Business Review on Change.* Harvard Business Review Paperback Series. Boston: Harvard Business School Press, 1998.

The *Harvard Business Review* paperback series is designed to bring today's managers and professionals the fundamental information they need to stay competitive in a fast-moving world. Here are the landmark ideas that have established the *Harvard Business Review* as required reading for ambitious businesspeople in organizations around the globe. From the seminal article "Leading Change" by John Kotter to Paul Strebel on "Why Do Employees Resist Change?" this collection is the most comprehensive resource available for embracing corporate change—and using it to your company's greatest advantage.

Harvard Business School Publishing. *Harvard Business Review on Leadership. Harvard Business Review* Paperback Series. Boston: Harvard Business School Press, 1998.

This collection gathers together eight of the *Harvard Business Review*'s most influential articles on leadership, challenging many long-held assumptions about the true sources of power and authority.

Harvard Business School Publishing. *How to Keep Your Employees Motivated, Productive, and Loyal. Harvard Business Review* Collection. Boston: Harvard Business School Publishing, 1999.

The collection includes "An Uneasy Look at Performance Appraisal" (Douglas McGregor and Warren G. Bennis); "Pygmalion in Management" (J. Sterling Livingston), "The Set-Up-To-Fail Syndrome" (Jean-Francois Manzoni and Jean-Louis Barsoux), "One More Time: How Do You Motivate Employees?" (Frederick Herzberg), "The Power of Predictability" (Howard H. Stevenson and Mihnea C. Moldoveanu), and "Nobody Trusts the Boss Completely—Now What?" (Fernando Bartolomé).

Harvard Business School Publishing. *Motivating Others to Follow. Harvard Business Review* OnPoint Collection. Boston: Harvard Business School Publishing, 2000.

This *Harvard Business Review* OnPoint collection suggests that there are three factors in the motivational equation: the power dynamics between the manager and the managed, the emotional intelligence or maturity of the manager, and the manager's own definition of success.

Ronald A. Heifetz. *Leadership without Easy Answers.* Cambridge, MA: The Belknap Press of Harvard University Press, 1994.

In this acclaimed book, Heifetz lays out his innovative concepts of adaptive leadership by examining the leadership roles of Lyndon Johnson, Martin Luther King Jr., Mohandas Gandhi, and others. He explores their sophisticated techniques for creating holding environments, using conflict to provoke change, and giving work back to the people.

John P. Kotter. *Leading Change.* Boston: Harvard Business School Press, 1996.

The author examines the efforts of more than 100 companies to remake themselves into better competitors. He identifies the most common mistakes leaders and managers make in attempting to create change and offers an eight-step process for overcoming obstacles and carrying out a firm's agenda: establishing a greater sense of urgency, creating the guiding coalition, developing a vision and strategy, communicating the change vision, empowering others to act, creating short-term wins, consolidating gains and producing even more change, and institutionalizing new approaches in the future.

Morgan W. McCall, Jr. *High Flyers: Developing the Next Generation of Leaders*. Boston: Harvard Business School Press, 1997.

The author offers an alternative to the conventional view of executive development as a fairly systematic process of identifying the right competencies and then selecting the right individuals. In place of the competency approach, McCall proposes a developmental model for growing executive talent that places utmost importance on experience as the linchpin of development. The ability to learn from experience, coupled with exposure to appropriate experience, creates an opportunity to learn executive skills. He offers numerous recommendations and interventions that will improve the probability that people will actually learn from experience—and remain open to continuous learning and development throughout their careers.

Bob Nelson and Burton Morris. *1001 Ways to Energize Employees*. New York: Workman Publishing Company, 1996.

This wonderfully entertaining collection of real-life examples shows how creative leaders motivate others. It will inspire even the weariest manager with practical ideas that can be implemented quickly and simply.

Robert E. Staub II. *The Heart of Leadership: 12 Practices of Courageous Leaders.* Provo, UT: Executive Excellence Publishing, 1996.

This book offers a practical and thorough examination of 12 practices of effective leaders. Staub intersperses advice from top leaders with plenty of lists, comparisons, and how-to information.

David Ulrich, Jack Zenger, and Norman Smallwood. *Results-Based Leadership.* Boston: Harvard Business School Press, 1999.

A landmark book, *Results-Based Leadership* challenges the conventional wisdom surrounding leadership. Authors Ulrich, Zenger, and Smallwood—world-renowned experts in human resources and training—argue that it is not enough to gauge leaders by personal traits such as character, style, and values. Rather, effective leaders know how to connect these leadership attributes with results.

Gary Yukl. *Leadership in Organizations.* 5th ed. Upper Saddle River: NJ, Prentice Hall, 2002.

A comprehensive text on the theory and practice of leadership, including topics such as effective leadership behavior, power and influence, types of leadership, strategic leadership, team leadership, ethical issues, cross-cultural leadership, and managing diversity.

eLearning Products

Harvard Business School Publishing. *Influencing and Motivating Others.* Boston: Harvard Business School Publishing, 2001. Online program.

Have you ever noticed how some people seem to have a natural ability to stir people to action? *Influencing and Motivating Others* provides actionable lessons on getting better results from direct reports (influencing performance), greater cooperation from your peers (lateral leadership), and stronger support from your own boss and senior management (persuasion). Managers will learn the secrets of "lateral leadership" (leading peers), negotiation and persuasion skills, and how to distinguish between effective and ineffective motivation methods. Through interactive cases, expert guidance, and activities for immediate application at work, this program helps managers to assess their ability to effectively persuade others, measure motivation skills, and enhance employee performance.

Harvard Business School Publishing. *Leadership Transitions.* Boston: Harvard Business School Publishing, 2001. Online program.

Whether taking on a new position in your current company or starting in a new organization, *Leadership Transitions* will help you succeed. This performance support resource, built with the expertise of Michael Watkins, prepares managers with the knowledge they need when they need it. Managers will learn to diagnose situations, assess vulnerabilities, accelerate learning, prioritize to succeed, work with a new boss, build teams, create partnerships, and align units. The program consists of a wide array of assessments and planning tools that learners can use throughout a transition period.

Harvard Business School Publishing. *What Is a Leader?* Boston: Harvard Business School Publishing, 2001. Online program.

What Is a Leader? is the most tangible, relevant online leadership program available on the market today. You will actively and immediately apply concepts to help you grow from a competent manager to an exceptional leader. Use this program to assess your ability to lead your organization through fundamental change, evaluate your leadership skills by examining how you allocate your time, and analyze your emotional intelligence to determine your strengths and weaknesses as a leader. In addition, work through interactive, real-world scenarios to determine what approach to take when diagnosing problems, learn to manage and even use the stress associated with change, empower others, and practice empathy when managing the human side of interactions. Based on the research and writings of John Kotter, author of *Leading Change*, and other of today's top leadership experts, this program is essential study for anyone charged with setting the direction of—and providing the motivation for—a modern organization.

Sources

We would like to acknowledge the sources that aided in developing this topic.

Lloyd Baird, professor, School of Management, and faculty director, Leadership Institute, Boston University

Warren G. Bennis, professor of business administration, University of Southern California

Larry Bird, basketball player and coach, NBA

Loren Gary, editor, *Harvard Management Update*

Daniel Goleman, consultant and psychologist

Douglas T. Hall, director of the Executive Development Roundtable, Boston University

Rakesh Khurana, assistant professor of organizational behavior, Harvard Business School

Hara Estroff Marano, editor-at-large, *Psychology Today*

Gordon Sullivan, Chief of Staff, U.S. Army (retired)

Andrew Young, U.N. Ambassador; Mayor of Atlanta, Georgia; Civil Rights Leader

Gary Yukl, professor, School of Business, State University of New York at Albany

Tools and Resources for Managing Crises

The "10 Worst Things That Could Happen" List

Some managers find it helpful to create and have available a list of the ten worst things that could happen at work and what they would do about them. Use this tool to record your own list or have a team or work group develop their list.

Situation	What I/We Would Do About It
1.	
2.	
3.	
4.	
5.	
6.	
7.	
8.	
9.	
10.	

Emergency Contact List

Be sure to include all internal and external people who need to be notified during a crisis.

Name:				
Home Address:				
Work Phone	**Home Phone**	**Cell Phone**	**E-mail Address**	**Fax Number**

Name:				
Home Address:				
Work Phone	**Home Phone**	**Cell Phone**	**E-mail Address**	**Fax Number**

Name:				
Home Address:				
Work Phone	**Home Phone**	**Cell Phone**	**E-mail Address**	**Fax Number**

Name:				
Home Address:				
Work Phone	**Home Phone**	**Cell Phone**	**E-mail Address**	**Fax Number**

Name:				
Home Address:				
Work Phone	**Home Phone**	**Cell Phone**	**E-mail Address**	**Fax Number**

Name:				
Home Address:				
Work Phone	**Home Phone**	**Cell Phone**	**E-mail Address**	**Fax Number**

Name:				
Home Address:				
Work Phone	**Home Phone**	**Cell Phone**	**E-mail Address**	**Fax Number**

Name:				
Home Address:				
Work Phone	**Home Phone**	**Cell Phone**	**E-mail Address**	**Fax Number**

Name:				
Home Address:				
Work Phone	**Home Phone**	**Cell Phone**	**E-mail Address**	**Fax Number**

Name:				
Home Address:				
Work Phone	**Home Phone**	**Cell Phone**	**E-mail Address**	**Fax Number**

Name:				
Home Address:				
Work Phone	**Home Phone**	**Cell Phone**	**E-mail Address**	**Fax Number**

Name:				
Home Address:				
Work Phone	**Home Phone**	**Cell Phone**	**E-mail Address**	**Fax Number**

Additional Notes

Precrisis Resource Planning

What can you do now to make things easier later? Use this checklist to brainstorm about resources you might need in the event of a potential crisis. This information can also form the basis for a crisis action plan.

Describe the Crisis

Resources Required

Money
How much money would be needed? _____ Person in charge? _____
In what form? _____ What can be done now? _____
How will it be accessed? _____ _____

Medical Help
Who or where? _____ Person in charge? _____
Insurance information? _____ What can be done now? _____
How to contact? _____ _____

Transportation
Type of transportation? _____ From where to where? _____
For what purpose? _____ Under what likely conditions? _____
For how many? _____ Person in charge? _____
For whom? _____ What can be done now? _____

Legal Help
Name of law firm or attorney? _____ Person in charge? _____
Type of legal help? _____ What can be done now? _____

Temporary Help
Skills needed? _____ Length of employment? _____
Name of agency? _____ Person in charge? _____
Number of people? _____ What can be done now? _____

Governmental Help
Name of agency? _____ Person in charge? _____
Name and number of contact? _____ What can be done now? _____

Media Help
Designated spokesperson? _____ Person in charge? _____
Public relations agency? _____ What can be done now? _____
Media insider? _____ _____

Other Required Resources

Scenario Impact Assessment

Use this form to explore the potential consequences of a crisis. By thinking through a scenario and exploring "what-if" situations, you can better prepare to act with confidence if that situation or crisis should arise. Be sure to concentrate first or most on high-risk situations.

Identify a high-level crisis according to the following assessment:

High-risk-level crisis = high impact on the company plus high probability of occurring

	LOW	MEDIUM	HIGH
Potential impact of crisis on company	☐	☐	☐
Probability of crisis occurring	☐	☐	☐
Risk level of crisis	☐	☐	☐

Briefly Describe the Scenario

What could happen? _____

Who would be involved? _____

Where? _____

What would be the worst possible consequences? _____

What is the probability that this situation will occur? _____

Assess the Risk Level of the Scenario

How much does this situation have the potential to:	Rating Low 1 2 3 4 5 High
Endanger the health or safety of others?	
Cause loss of life and/or long-term harm to human health?	
Cause harm to the environment?	
Affect business-as-usual in your department or your business?	
Damage your department or your business's industry or public reputation?	
Have a significant financial impact?	
Trigger negative media attention, legal action, or governmental scrutiny?	
Damage employee relations or morale or contribute to employee turnover?	

List Other Potential Negative Impacts

Implications for Action

Given your responses to the above set of questions, are there certain preventative actions that can be taken now to lessen the negative impact of this scenario? Is there a plan in place to deal effectively and decisively with the worst consequences?

Capturing Learning from the Crisis

When the crisis is finally over, it's tempting to just put the whole thing behind you and move on. But a valuable learning opportunity will be lost. Use this form to capture some of the learning that you, your team, division, or company gleaned from experiencing the crisis. Break down each problem you faced, how you handled it, and what you learned. Then figure out how to prevent a similar problem from reoccurring and/or how to respond to it more effectively.

Crisis or Problem	Action Taken	What We Learned	Preventative Action
Example: *Key executive suddenly left to join another company.*	*We rushed into a disorganized search for a replacement.*	*We were unprepared and didn't know what our criteria were in our search. The process took too long.*	*Develop a succession plan for every key position in the company.*

Summary

In what ways did we handle the crisis effectively? How can we be sure to incorporate these positive actions into our crisis-management plans?

In what ways did we mishandle the crisis? What were the negative effects of our actions? How can we improve our crisis management in the future?

Test Yourself

This section offers ten multiple-choice questions to help you identify your baseline knowledge of crisis-management essentials. Answers to the questions are given at the end of the test.

1. You've just been assigned the task of preventing crises that could cause great harm to your organization. What's the first thing you do?

    a. Identify the crises that would cause most harm.

    b. Identify the crises that would be most likely.

    c. Form a crisis-analysis team.

2. A key employee has just informed you that his wife has a terminal illness. After expressing your sympathy and concern, what do you do?

    a. Find out how long she is expected to live.

    b. Work with him and other employees to create a flexible work plan.

    c. Encourage him to take a leave of absence.

3. True or false: When you are analyzing the potential damage a crisis can cause, the bottom line is the most important factor to consider.

    a. True.

    b. False.

4. What percentage of companies that experience a major data loss survive that crisis?

   a. Less than 10 percent.

   b. Between 10 percent and 30 percent.

   c. More than 30 percent.

5. Which type of crisis actually contains the greatest potential for business opportunity?

   a. A public-safety disaster.

   b. A technological breakdown.

   c. A market swing.

6. An internal accountant informs you that your highly paid staff member (with whom you have a friendly relationship) may be embezzling small sums of money. What do you do?

   a. Tell the accountant that the employee makes too much money to steal such small amounts.

   b. Discuss the situation with the employee offline, as a subtle warning to stop the embezzling in case it happens to be true.

   c. Examine the books closely with the accountant. If something's amiss, call in an auditor.

7. Which of the following organizational cultures would likely be most responsive to and effective in handling a crisis?

   a. A competitive culture where decisions get made and the job gets done no matter what.

b. A friendly culture based on trust.

c. A culture where information is closely protected and decisions are made at the top.

8. A disaster has just struck your company, and you are the designated spokesperson. A press conference will take place in one hour. How are you and your staff preparing to handle it?

a. You are writing a carefully worded statement revealing only what is about to become public knowledge.

b. You are writing a confident stating putting the most positive outlook on the problem and solutions.

c. You are preparing honest answers to the five questions you would least like to be asked.

9. You are the project manager on a key product for your company. Early results from user testing are mixed. You must still deliver within your deadline and on budget, but you don't know what to do about the mixed results. What is your first step?

a. Set up a flexible production team that can quickly make changes to the product indicated by focus tests.

b. Step back from the project. Analyze the information you're getting, to see what the problem really is.

c. Continue supporting the vision that began development of the product. Go about business as usual, creating an atmosphere of confidence and calm.

10. A crisis is finally over, and everyone feels both relieved and weary. Though you're tempted to get on with life, you know that you must assess what went wrong in order to prevent it from happening again. Where do you start?

  a. Get input from everyone involved to create a plan for the future.

  b. Determine who caused the problem and discipline him or her.

  c. Work with one or two key players to create a plan for the future.

Answers to test questions

1, c. Putting together a crisis-analysis team comprising a group of experienced people with different perspectives will give you an excellent start. Make the team a formal one with assigned tasks. A "watercooler" chat will not give you the depth or breadth you need to prevent and manage crises.

2, b. Your employee may want and need to work during the crisis, and may be very capable of performing on a part-time basis. Bringing people together during this crisis can help create the emotional support your employee will need to get through it.

3, b. A crisis has the potential to damage the health and safety of employees, your company's reputation, and your ability to serve customers—all equal in importance to the organization's bottom line.

4, a. A University of Texas study found that only 6 percent of companies that undergo major data loss survive the crisis. The good news is that this is one crisis that an organization can avoid relatively easily.

5, c. Changes in the market can spell disaster *or* growth for a company, depending on how well the organization predicts and handles such changes.

6, c. By examining the books with your accountant and calling in an independent auditor if something is amiss, you investigate the facts as quickly and objectively as possible—which is important to do in any crisis.

7, b. A company that values trust and compassion and that has created informal networks for the exchange of information can most easily demonstrate the team spirit and open communication needed to survive a crisis.

8, c. People are going to ask you tough questions whether you like it or not. You're better off being prepared with honest answers, even if the answer is "I don't know."

9, b. You can't solve a problem until you've clearly identified what it is. Once you've isolated the problem, you can break it down into component parts and decide how to resolve the situation.

10, a. Everyone who was affected by the crisis has a valuable perspective on what went wrong and ideas for how to prevent a similar crisis. Get input from all these individuals before making new plans.

To Learn More

Articles

Argenti, Paul. "Crisis Communication: Lessons from 9/11." *Harvard Business Review* (December 2002).

> In this article, executives from a range of industries talk about how their companies, including Morgan Stanley, Oppenheimer Funds, American Airlines, Verizon, the New York Times, Dell, and Starbucks, went about restoring operations and morale after the terrorist attack of 9/11. From his interviews with these individuals, author and management professor Paul Argenti was able to distill a number of lessons, each of which, he says, may "serve as guideposts for any company facing a crisis that undermines its employees' composure, confidence, or concentration."

Augustine, Norman R. "Reshaping an Industry: Lockheed Martin's Survival Story." *Harvard Business Review* (November–December 1997).

> In this behind-the-scenes story about the effects of the end of the Cold War on industry, Augustine draws important lessons about what industries can do to avoid crises and manage them once they begin.

Harvard Business School Publishing. "How to Keep a Crisis from Happening." *Harvard Management Update* (December 2000).

This article contains concise, practical information on how to prevent a crisis and how to handle one while it's occurring.

Harvard Business School Publishing. "Managing a Crisis." *Harvard Management Update* (August 2005).

This article explores the three emotions that combine during a crisis: fear of disaster, anticipation of a potentially positive outcome, and a desire for the crisis to be over. Each pulls you in a different emotional direction; together they create a distinct feeling of stress. And under stress, you feel the pressure to make a decision. But the pressure can push you to make decisions solely to be "doing something." Thus, people often respond to crises in ways that can aggravate rather than relieve the crisis. The authors explain how to avoid these futile and often harmful responses.

Mitroff, Ian I., and Murat C. Alpaslan. "Preparing for Evil." *Harvard Business Review* (April 2003).

The authors show how crisis-prepared companies use a systematic approach to focus their efforts. In addition to planning for natural disasters, they divide man-made calamities into two sorts: accidental ones, like the *Exxon Valdez* oil spill, and deliberate ones, like product tampering. Then they take steps to broaden their thinking about such potential crises. They imagine themselves as terrorists, for instance, or consider threats that would be common in other industries. And they seek creative outside input from investigative journalists, lawyers, and even reformed criminals.

Books

Deming, W. Edwards. *Out of the Crisis.* Cambridge, MA: MIT Press, 2000.

According to W. Edwards Deming, American companies require nothing less than a transformation of management style and of governmental relations with industry. In *Out of the Crisis*, originally published in 1986, Deming offers a theory of management based on his famous 14 Points for Management. Management's failure to plan for the future, he claims, brings about loss of market, which brings about loss of jobs. Management must be judged not only by the quarterly dividend, but by innovative plans to stay in business, protect investment, ensure future dividends, and provide more jobs through improved product and service. In simple, direct language, he explains the principles of management transformation and how to apply them.

Grove, Andrew S. *Only the Paranoid Survive: How to Exploit the Crisis Points That Challenge Every Company.* New York: Bantam Books, 1999.

Andrew Grove, chairman of Intel Corporation, outlines his inside experience and the ups and downs of Intel. He gives the reader a great inside look at the way change from every quarter can affect a major corporation, and he shares his vision in practical, direct language for capitalizing on change and crisis.

Harvard Business School Publishing. *Harvard Business Review on Crisis Management*. Boston: Harvard Business School Press, 1999.

This collection of eight essays highlights leading ideas on how to deal with difficult situations, crises, and other sensitive topics in a business environment. Obtaining the managerial skills and tools to effectively manage or avoid these crises is critical to the survival and success of your organization. In the lead article, "Managing the Crisis You Tried to Prevent," Norman Augustine uses his extensive personal experience in many executive situations to break down crises into predictable stages, with advice on how to handle each one. Other articles in this compilation give practical advice from frontline people on such topics as layoffs, product recalls, executive defection, media policy, and leadership.

Hurst, David K. *Crisis and Renewal: Meeting the Challenge of Organizational Change*. Boston: Harvard Business School Press, 2002.

Hurst presents a radically different view of how organizations evolve and renew themselves. The author tracks a cross-section of enterprises from their creative beginnings through the institutionalization of their success. Using a model of organizational ecocycles, he argues that managers need to create deliberate crises to preserve their organizations from destruction and to renew them with creativity and meaning.

Sources

We would like to acknowledge the sources we used in developing this topic.

Augustine, Norman R. "50 Signs of Trouble—A List by Norman Augustine." Unpublished.

Augustine, Norman R. "Managing the Crisis You Tried to Prevent." *Harvard Business Review* OnPoint Enhanced Edition (2002).

Augustine, Norman R. Personal communication. November 2001.

Bureau of Labor Statistics.

Carlone, Katie. Personal communication. January 2002.

Dutton, Jane E., Peter J. Frost, Monica C. Worline, Jacoba M. Lilius, and Jason M. Kanov. "Leading in Times of Trauma." *Harvard Business Review* (January–February 2002).

Fink, Steven. *Crisis Management—Planning for the Inevitable.* New York: American Management Association, 1986.

Harvard Business School Publishing. *Manager's Toolkit.* Boston: Harvard Business School Press, 2004.

"How to Keep a Crisis from Happening." *Harvard Management Update* (December 2000).

Mitroff, Ian I., Christine M. Pearson, and L. Katharine Harrington. *The Essential Guide to Managing Corporate Crises.* Oxford: Oxford University Press, 1996.

"Read This, Then Go Back Up Your Data." *Fortune,* Special Tech Edition (Winter 2002).

Silva, Michael, and Terry McGann. *Overdrive—Managing in Crisis-Filled Times.* New York: John Wiley & Sons, 1995.

Sontag, Sherry, and Christopher Drew. "Blind Man's Bluff: The Untold Story of American Submarine Espionage." *Public Affairs* (1998).

Van Der Heijden, Kees. *Scenarios—The Art of Strategic Conversation.* New York: John Wiley & Sons, 1996.

Vernon, Lillian, with Catherine Fredman. "Too Much of a Good Thing." *United Airlines Hemispheres* (November 2001).

Vogelstein, Fred. "Can Schwab Get Its Mojo Back?" *Fortune* (September 17, 2001).

Wack, Pierre. "Scenarios: Uncharted Waters Ahead." *Harvard Business Review* (September–October 1985).

Tools and Resources
for Making Decisions

Setting the Stage

Use this worksheet to think through how you will approach the decision-making process.

Description of Decision

Describe a decision that you and your group needs to make:

Participants

List the names and roles of the people you will include in your decision-making group. Identify key stakeholders, experts, and opponents (individuals who may oppose the decision or block its implementation).

Time

How much time is available to make this decision? Does the decision need to be made by a specific date?

Setting

Where will you meet? (If possible, consider using a location that is different from your usual meeting place.)

Decision-Making Approach

Which approach will you use to make the decision: consensus, majority vote, qualified consensus, directive leadership, or a combination? (Consider the importance and implications of the decision. You may need to reserve the final decision for yourself.) How will you make the choice if the group reaches an impasse?

Climate

List some questions you might ask to encourage debate:

Anticipate some positions on the proposed courses of action that are up for decision.

How will you strike a balance between advocacy- and inquiry-based debate?

Brainstorming Planning

Use this worksheet to prepare for a brainstorming session. Consider the parameters for planning the meeting carefully.

Description of issue/problem:	Date of session:

Who needs to attend:	Why? Special knowledge/skills they contribute?

Materials needed, including:

☐ Flip chart, markers   ☐ Equipment
☐ Easel   ☐ Visuals
☐ Masking tape   ☐ Information handouts
☐ Small notes with a sticky backing   ☐ Other:

Session planning:

☐ Opening, warm-up activity
☐ Structured or unstructured brainstorming process
☐ Who will act as recorder
☐ After the session, who will follow up and report to the group
☐ Opposing views to anticipate

Ground rules: For best results, remember to ...

1. Limit the group's size to between 5 and 15 (though any size group can brainstorm).
2. Assign a neutral facilitator to guide the session.
3. Explain to the group that position and rank play no role during the session.
4. Explain that "reality testing" and forming judgments are not part of the brainstorming session. (All ideas and answers are to be accepted without dispute, criticism, or correction.)
5. Write the problem/issue to brainstorm on a chalkboard or flip chart where everyone can see it throughout the session.
6. Seek agreement from everyone that the issue is stated correctly and precisely.
7. On the chalkboard or flip chart, record all ideas. (Or members may call out ideas, then write them on notes and stick them on the idea board.)
8. Sort the ideas and answers into categories or general groupings. (The group may then sort through and rate or rank order ideas.)
9. After the session, summarize the brainstorming outcomes; report findings to all participants in the group.

Evaluating Alternatives

Use this tool to help you think through your alternatives.

Defining Alternatives

Describe the decision you are trying to make.
Step back and be sure that you are thinking about the root cause of the problem.

List the decision-making objectives your group identified. What criteria will you use to judge success?
Be specific about your goals and quantify wherever possible.

What are some of the most promising alternatives your team explored?
Remember to consider blending alternatives into better solutions.

Evaluating Your Alternatives

For each of the alternatives listed above, write down the factors that are important to consider when making your decision. These factors include:

- **Costs:** How much will the alternative cost? Will it result in cost savings now or over the long term? Are there any hidden costs? Are there likely to be additional costs down the road? Does this alternative meet budget constraints?

- **Benefits:** What kind of profits will we realize if we implement this alternative? Will it increase the quality of our product? Will customer satisfaction increase?

- **Intangibles:** Will our reputation improve if we implement this alternative? Will our customers and/or employees be more loyal?

- **Time:** How long will it take to implement this alternative? Could there be delays? If so, what impact will this have on any schedules?

- **Feasibility:** Can this alternative be implemented realistically? Are there any obstacles that must be overcome? If this alternative is implemented, what resistance might be encountered inside or outside of the organization?

- **Resources:** How many people are needed to implement this alternative? Are they available? What other projects will suffer if individuals focus on this option?

- **Risks:** What are the risks associated with this alternative? For example, could this option result in loss of profits or competitive advantage? Will competitors respond? If so, how?

- **Ethics:** Is this alternative legal? Is it in the best interests of the customers, the employees, and the community where we operate? Would I feel comfortable if other people knew about this alternative?

Alternative 1:

Relevant factors:

Alternative 2:

Relevant factors:

Alternative 3:

Relevant factors:

Communications Notification Form

Once you make a decision, you need to communicate it to those responsible for implementing it and to everyone affected by it. Use this form to keep track of the people you need to inform and to outline what you plan to tell them.

Part I. Who needs to be informed of the decision that's been made?

Those Responsible for Implementation

Name and title	Date to be informed and method	Tasks to be assigned, if applicable
Example: Janet Doe, Product Manager	*In-person meeting to review market study and proposed products by 12/1*	*Janet Doe's team to develop plan for new products*

Other Stakeholders and Department Heads

Name and title	Date to be informed and method	Tasks to be assigned, if applicable
Example: Jonathan Smith, Director, Product Management	*E-mail John before 12/1 to let him know you will be working with Janet Doe and her team*	*None*

External Constituents and Customers		
Name and title	Date to be informed and method	Tasks to be assigned, if applicable
Example: Reseller Network	*Send out new-product announcement and collateral before 2/15*	*Identify any seller concerns*

Part II. What needs to be communicated about the decision that's been made?

1. Describe the issue or circumstances that required a decision. Think about this from your stakeholders' perspective.

2. List your objectives, or desired outcomes, in making the decision.

3. List the participants who were involved in making the decision.

4. Briefly explain some of the alternatives that were considered.

5. Discuss the final decision that was reached and its benefit to the stakeholder.

6. Outline the implementation plan and time frame.

7. Recognize those who were involved in the decision-making process.

8. Solicit feedback and comments on the outcome.

Assessing the Decision-Making Process

*Use this tool to assess how well you and your team support
an effective decision-making process.*

	Rating		
Questions about yourself	**All of the Time**	**Some of the Time**	**Never**
1. Do you make sure that the group's objectives in the decision making are clear from the start?			
2. Do you seek out information from a variety of people and sources to make decisions?			
3. Do you frame issues in a way that encourages the exploration of multiple solutions?			
4. Do you make sure that at least one minority viewpoint is considered in all group discussions?			
5. Do you use reliable data and statistics to support your arguments?			
6. Do you involve knowledgeable outsiders to participate in group discussions to provide insight?			
7. Do you encourage team members to step out of their traditional roles when generating alternatives?			
8. Do you facilitate open, constructive dialogue?			
9. Do you ask probing, open-ended questions to promote understanding and the creation of new alternatives?			
10. Do you continually review your objectives during your meetings to ensure that your discussions are on target?			

	Rating		
Questions about your group	**All of the Time**	**Some of the Time**	**Never**
11. Does everyone in the group participate?			
12. Do group members listen attentively to the viewpoints of others?			
13. Do group members act more like unbiased critical thinkers than advocates of particular interests?			
14. Does your group consider multiple alternatives for a decision?			
15. Does your group take time to ask questions and debate options before coming to agreement?			

Ideas for Improvement

On the basis of your answers, what changes could you make to your decision making to make it more effective? To your group's?

Test Yourself

This section offers ten multiple-choice questions to help you identify your baseline knowledge of decision-making essentials. Answers to the questions are given at the end of the test.

1. Which of the following approaches is likely to lead to excessive group harmony?

  a. Suggest a possible solution in an early meeting to get the group to consider a new idea.

  b. Use the point-counterpoint technique in an early meeting to encourage debate.

  c. Ask someone in an early meeting who hasn't yet participated to make a comment or suggestion.

2. Which of the following is a sign that your discussions may have deteriorated into advocacy mode?

  a. A team member is asking a lot of probing questions of her colleagues at every meeting.

  b. Participants are explaining their viewpoints to each other in the hallways before and after meetings.

  c. The minority viewpoint has generated a lot of conversation during meetings.

3. Which of the following teams would you assemble to choose a new software program to manage the inventory at your warehouse?

   a. Four people from purchasing, five information technology professionals, a warehouse floor supervisor, and a person from finance.

   b. Two people from purchasing, three information technology professionals, and a warehouse floor supervisor.

   c. Three people from purchasing and three information technology professionals.

4. Decide whether the following statement is true or false: creating a decision tree will identify the *best* choice for your problem.

   a. True.

   b. False.

5. Which of the following illustrates an *incorrect* way to facilitate a brainstorming session?

   a. Encourage participants to verbalize any ideas that come into their heads. Record their ideas on a flip chart for evaluation in a follow-up meeting.

   b. At the start of the meeting, ask participants to write down any ideas that come into their heads. Ask them to then share their ideas publicly. As they speak, write down their ideas on a flip chart.

   c. Encourage participants to verbalize any ideas that come into their heads. Discuss the merits of each idea with the group, and record the best ideas on a flip chart.

6. You want to outsource the manufacturing of a printed circuit board. Who is the best person to approach for initial advice?

a. A manager in another department who recently decided to keep manufacturing in-house.

b. A manager in another department who recently started to outsource its manufacturing.

c. A manager in another department who recently mentioned that she thinks outsourcing makes good financial sense.

7. Which of the following is the *best* way to frame an issue related to a high volume of customer complaints about a product?

a. "How can we change the product to increase customer satisfaction?"

b. "What is wrong with the product?"

c. "Why are customers dissatisfied?"

8. Which of the following is an example of the point-counter-point approach to decision making?

a. A manager asks each team member to come to a meeting prepared to present his or her ideas to the other group members. The group then discusses each proposal and tries to find a set of assumptions and recommendations that the group can accept.

b. A manager asks half of the group to come to a meeting prepared to present a proposal they created together to the other group members. The other half of the group critiques the proposal and presents its analysis. The whole group then tries to find a set of assumptions and recommendations that the group can accept.

c. A manager splits his team into two subgroups. He asks one subgroup to come to a meeting prepared to present a proposal; he asks the other subgroup to be prepared to present an opposing proposal. After both presentations have been made, the whole group tries to agree on a course of action.

9. Once you make a decision, what should you do next?

a. Assign reasonable and attainable tasks to your team and to anyone else who will need to implement the decision.

b. Create a work plan that outlines the tasks you will take to implement your decision.

c. Identify who should know about the decision.

10. Decide whether the following statement is true or false: if a decision is legal and maximizes profits, then it is an ethical course of action.

a. True.

b. False.

Answers to test questions

1, a. If you, as a manager, make a suggestion early in a meeting in the hopes of encouraging your team to consider other alternatives, your action can backfire. Employees may view the suggestion as your preferred solution and support the idea to try to please you. To avoid excessive group harmony, consider using a technique that encourages people to consider multiple options and to critique each other, such as point-counterpoint. Also encourage those individuals who are reluctant to participate to voice their opinions.

2, b. In an advocacy-based discussion, people try to persuade each other to support their viewpoints. Team members who are discussing their views in the hallway may be trying to convince others of the merits of their ideas. These individuals could influence others to see the decision process in terms of winners and losers—which doesn't lead to good decision making. On the other hand, if your team is asking probing questions and considering minority viewpoints, it is adopting the more inquiry-based approach essential to effective business decisions.

3, b. This group contains representatives from departments that will be affected by the change, and the team is a reasonable size. Unless you need a bigger group to accommodate a variety of perspectives, aim for five to seven participants in a decision-making team. Larger groups are more difficult to manage.

4, b. A decision tree will *not* necessarily point to the best solution. Instead, it provides a visual representation of the uncertainties and possible outcomes associated with a decision. Thus, it helps you evaluate your options. You will still need to assess the information in the decision tree to make your choice. Creating a prioritization matrix may help you evaluate your options at this stage.

5, c. Discussing the merits of each idea as it is offered will proba-bly *not* encourage brainstorming, because brainstorming should be used to generate alternatives—not to evaluate them as they're presented. When leading a brainstorming session, ask people to focus on identifying as many alternatives as possible rather than criticizing or debating ideas as they're presented. You can evaluate ideas later, after you've generated an exhaustive list of options.

6, a. A common mistake people make when considering a deci-sion is to seek information that supports their existing point of view and to ignore information that contradicts it. When faced with a decision, asking a colleague to argue against your potential decision may identify weaknesses that you haven't yet considered. Seeking only people who have similar views or who have made a similar decision is likely to strengthen your resolve to proceed without sufficiently careful consideration.

7, c. When trying to frame an issue, it's good to ask questions that encourage exploration and to avoid questions that assume the na-ture of the problem (such as "How can we change the product?" or "What's wrong with the product?"). Your goal is to get at the core of the issue before you begin examining possible solutions.

8, c. To use the point-counterpoint technique, you divide your team into two groups and ask them to develop opposing propos-als. After both groups present their proposals, the whole group tries to agree on a course of action. The point-counterpoint tech-nique—as well as a consensus approach and the intellectual-watchdog technique described in the other options—are all useful for encouraging team members to reach a final decision.

9, c. Once you make a decision, you need to determine who should know about it. You do not want to start implementing a decision until you are sure that the people who will be affected by the decision are aware of your plans. A common mistake is to make a decision with a team of people and then forget to inform others of the course of action that was chosen. While other people may not be directly involved in implementing your decision, they may still be affected by it.

10, b. Even though a decision may be legal, it is not necessarily the right thing to do. As a manager, you have a responsibility to consider ethics when making a decision. Your personal values and any corporate statements of social responsibility will guide you. Ultimately, you must balance the interests of all stakeholders, from those who will gain from a decision to those who could be adversely affected.

To Learn More

Articles

Bagley, Constance E. "The Ethical Leader's Decision Tree." *Harvard Business Review*, February 2003.

If you spring for optional pollution-control devices at your overseas plant, have you violated your duty to maximize shareholder value? This article provides a framework for exposing conflicts between corporate actions and corporate ethics that can help clarify ethical dilemmas—and potentially head off bad decisions.

Charan, Ram. "Conquering a Culture of Indecision." *Harvard Business Review* OnPoint Enhanced Edition, April 2002.

The single greatest cause of corporate underperformance is the failure to execute. Author Ram Charan, drawing on a quarter century of observing organizational behavior, perceives that such failures are caused by a misfire in the personal interactions that are supposed to produce results. The inability to take decisive action is rooted in a company's culture. But, Charan notes, since leaders create a culture of indecisiveness, they can also break it. This article provides guidance for leaders to move their organizations from paralysis to action.

Garvin, David, and Michael Roberto. "What You Don't Know About Making Decisions." *Harvard Business Review* OnPoint Enhanced Edition, November 2003.

The authors take a closer look at inquiry—a highly productive decision-making approach. When you balance advocacy with inquiry, you carefully consider a variety of options, work with others to discover the best solutions, and stimulate creative thinking rather than suppressing dissension. The payoff? High-quality decisions that advance your company's objectives and that you reach in a timely manner and implement effectively. But inquiry isn't easy. Garvin and Roberto explain how to manage the three keys to using inquiry: promoting constructive conflict, accepting ambiguity, and balancing *divergence* during early discussions with *unity* during implementation of the decision.

Hammond, John S., Ralph L. Keeney, and Howard Raiffa. "The Hidden Traps in Decision Making." *Harvard Business Review* OnPoint Enhanced Edition, November 2000.

The human mind is prone to distortions and biases that can undermine even the most well-thought-out decision-making process. This article examines eight psychological traps that are particularly likely to affect the way we make business decisions. The best way to avoid these traps is awareness—forewarned is forearmed. The authors also show executives how to take other simple steps to protect themselves and their organizations from various kinds of mental lapses.

Kim, W. Chan, and Renée A. Mauborgne, "Fair Process: Managing in the Knowledge Economy." *Harvard Business Review* OnPoint Enhanced Edition, February 2000.

Unlike the traditional factors of production—land, labor, and capital—knowledge is a resource that can't be forced out of people. But creating and sharing knowledge is essential to fostering innovation, the key challenge of the knowledge-based economy. To create a climate in which employees volunteer their creativity and expertise, managers need to look beyond the traditional tools at their disposal. They need to build trust. The authors have studied the links between trust, idea sharing, and corporate performance for more than a decade. They offer an explanation for why people resist change even when it would benefit them directly. In every case, the decisive factor was what the authors call fair process—fairness in the way a company makes and executes decisions. Fair process may sound like a soft issue, but it is crucial to building trust and unlocking ideas.

Luecke, Richard. "Make Better Decisions." *Harvard Management Update*, April 2006.

We know that individuals can be trained to make better decisions, but as greater authority is moved into the hands of frontline managers, developing a broadly based decision competency is becoming more important. Some corporations are taking steps to enhance organizational decision competence. Learn how two of these companies, General Motors and Chevron, developed programs for improving decision quality and how they got started.

Rogers, Paul, and Marcia Blenko. "Who Has the D? How Clear Decision Roles Enhance Organizational Performance." *Harvard Business Review* OnPoint Enhanced Edition, January 2006.

Decisions are the coin of the realm in business. But even in highly respected companies, decisions can get stuck inside the organization like loose change. As a result, the entire decision-making process can stall, usually at one of four bottlenecks: global versus local, center versus business unit, function versus function, and inside versus outside partners. Decision-making bottlenecks can occur whenever there is ambiguity or tension over who gets to decide what. For example, do marketers or product developers get to decide the features of a new product? Should a major capital investment depend on the approval of the business unit that will own it, or should headquarters make the final call? Bain consultants Paul Rogers and Marcia Blenko use an approach called RAPID (recommend, agree, perform, input, and decide) to help companies unclog their decision-making bottlenecks by explicitly defining roles and responsibilities. When revamping its decision-making process, a company must take some practical steps: align decision roles with the most important sources of value, make sure that decisions are made by the right people at the right levels of the organization, and let the people who will live with the new process help design it.

Books

Bazerman, Max H. *Judgment in Managerial Decision Making.* New York: John Wiley & Sons, 2002.

In situations requiring careful judgment, we're all influenced by our own biases. Bazerman's book provides a framework to help managers overcome those biases to make better decisions. Through the use of vivid real-world examples, Bazerman identifies systematic ways in which judgment and decision-making skills deviate from rationality under uncertain conditions. The book provides practical strategies and exercises for changing and improving your decision-making processes so they become part of your permanent behavior.

Garvin, David A. *General Management: Processes and Action.* Boston: McGraw-Hill, 2002.

Understanding the skills necessary to influence the design, direction, and functioning of management processes is essential to effective management. Focusing on implementation and the way general managers get things done, Garvin walks through management processes like strategic planning, business planning, decision making, and budgeting to help move an organization forward. Using real-world examples, Garvin illustrates a wide range of management processes and activities and their link to performance.

Janis, Irving L. *Victims of Groupthink.* Boston: Houghton Mifflin, 1972.

Using examples drawn from the American government, Janis tests his hypothesis that groups often tend to make more extreme decisions than individuals. From the Bay of Pigs invasion to the Watergate cover-up, Janis portrays in detail how group dynamics helped to put participants on a disastrous course and keep them there. In addition, Janis presents fresh ideas on how and why groupthink occurs, and offers suggestions for avoiding it.

eLearning Programs

Harvard Business School Publishing. *Case in Point.* Boston: Harvard Business School Publishing, 2004.

Case in Point is a flexible set of online cases, designed to help prepare middle- and senior-level managers for a variety of leadership challenges. These short, reality-based scenarios provide sophisticated content to create a focused view into the realities of the life of a leader. Your managers will experience Aligning Strategy, Removing Implementation Barriers, Overseeing Change, Anticipating Risk, Ethical Decisions, Building a Business Case, Cultivating Customer Loyalty, Emotional Intelligence, Developing a Global Perspective, Fostering Innovation, Defining Problems, Selecting Solutions, Managing Difficult Interactions, The Coach's Role, Delegating for Growth, Managing Creativity, Influencing Others, Managing Performance, Providing Feedback, and Retaining Talent.

Harvard Business School Publishing. *Decision Making.* Boston: Harvard Business School Publishing, 2002.

Based on research and writings of leadership experts, this program examines the frameworks for making decisions, decision-making biases, and the role of intuition in this context.

Increase the decision-making confidence in an organization by equipping managers with the interactive lessons, expert guidance, and activities for immediate application at work. Managers will learn to recognize the role intuition plays in decision making, apply a process to complicated decisions, identify and avoid thinking traps, simplify complex decisions, and tackle fast decision making.

Harvard Business School Publishing. *Managing Difficult Conversations*. Boston: Harvard Business School Publishing, 2001.

This program will help you understand why disagreements occur and help you build conclusions collaboratively. These productive dialogue skills will lead to a more accurate, shared understanding of the information exchanged in your daily interactions. *Managing Difficult Conversations* examines techniques for approaching and handling difficult business conversations. The program explores how mental models influence our private thinking and, thus, our behavior. It presents the Left-Hand Column exercise as a technique for unveiling and examining our internal thought process. The program also examines five unproductive thinking habits that many people fall into during difficult conversations and five productive alternative ways of thinking. By examining your own thinking habits and actively seeking more productive mind-sets, you can learn to approach difficult conversations with confidence, avoid blaming, overcome defensiveness, and make better business decisions.

Harvard Business School Publishing. *Productive Business Dialogue*.

Boston: Harvard Business School Publishing, 2002.

This program shows managers how to craft conversations that are fact based, minimize defensiveness, and draw out the best thinking from everyone involved. *Productive Business Dialogue* introduces the Ladder of Inference, a tool that helps participants in a dialogue understand the distinctions among fact, interpretation, and conclusions and how making these distinctions clear can dramatically enhance the productivity of meetings and discussions. Through interactive, real-world scenarios, you will practice shaping interactions that maximize learning and lead to better-informed decisions.

Sources

The following sources aided in development of this book:

Bagley, Constance E. "The Ethical Leader's Decision Tree." *Harvard Business Review*, February 2003.

Bazerman, Max H. *Judgment in Managerial Decision Making.* New York: John Wiley & Sons, 2002.

Cadbury, Sir Adrian. "Ethical Managers Make Their Own Rules." *Harvard Business Review*, September–October 1987.

Charan, Ram. "Conquering a Culture of Indecision." *Harvard Business Review*, April 2001.

Crowe, Mattison. "Why the Members of Your Team Won't Speak Up, and What You Can Do About It." *Harvard Management Update*, November 1996.

Drucker, Peter F. "The Effective Decision." *Harvard Business Review*, January–February 1967.

Garvin, David A. *General Management: Processes and Action.* Boston: McGraw-Hill, 2002.

Garvin, David A., and Michael A. Roberto. "What You Don't Know About Making Decisions." *Harvard Business Review* OnPoint Enhanced Edition, September 2001.

Gary, Loren. "Cognitive Bias: Systemic Errors in Decision

Making." *Harvard Management Update*, April 1998.

Gary, Loren. "Problem Solving for Decision Makers." *Harvard Management Update*, December 1997.

Hammond, John S., Ralph L. Keeney, and Howard Raiffa. "Even Swaps: A Rational Method for Making Trade-offs." *Harvard Business Review*, March–April 1998.

Hammond, John S., Ralph L. Keeney, and Howard Raiffa. "The Hidden Traps in Decision Making." *Harvard Business Review*, September–October 1998.

Janis, Irving L. *Victims of Groupthink*. Boston: Houghton Mifflin, 1972.

Kim, W. Chan, and Renée A. Mauborgne. "Fair Process: Managing in the Knowledge Economy." *Harvard Business Review*, February 2000.

Magee, John F. "Decision Trees for Decision Making." *Harvard Business Review*, July–August 1964.

Morgan, Nick. "Put Your Decision Making to the Test: Communicate." *Harvard Management Communication Letter*, November 2001.

Straus, David, and Pat Milton. "Collaborative Decision Making." *Development*, July 2003.

About the Subject Experts

Lloyd Baird, Subject Expert, Leading People

Lloyd Baird is Professor of Management at Boston University and Chair of the Organizational Behavior Department. He is also currently a principal at the Systems Research Center and Research Director of the Executive Development Roundtable, which focuses on the role of executives and leadership development. Dr. Baird works with corporations on issues such as the risks and potential of corporate-wide learning, knowledge, and leadership initiatives as well as with executives to help them drive both personal and organization transformation. He received his BS degree from Utah State University and his MBA and PhD from Michigan State University.

Norman R. Augustine, Subject Expert, Managing Crises

Norman R. Augustine is chairman of the Executive Committee, Lockheed Martin; he formerly served as chairman and CEO of Lockheed Martin Corporation; director of Black & Decker, Phillips Petroleum, and Procter & Gamble; and undersecretary for the U.S. Army during the Vietnam War. He is the author of *Augustine's Laws* (Viking Penguin, 1986) and "Managing the Crisis You Tried to Prevent" (*Harvard Business Review*, 1995).

David A. Garvin, Subject Expert, Making Decisions

David A. Garvin is the C. Roland Christensen Professor of Business Administration at Harvard Business School, where he specializes in leadership and general management. For more than twenty-five years, he has studied and taught the principles of organizational learning, business and management processes, and the design and leadership of large, complex organizations. He is the author or coauthor of nine books, including *General Management: Processes and Action, Learning in Action, Education for Judgment,* and *Managing Quality,* as well as thirty articles and eight videotape series. He is a three-time winner of the McKinsey Award, given annually for the best article in *Harvard Business Review.*